RAW
POTLUCK

over
100
simply delicious
raw dishes for
everyday
entertaining

THE COMPLETE BOOK OF RAW FOOD

RAW POTLUCK

over 100 simply delicious raw dishes for everyday entertaining

Lisa Montgomery

hatherleigh

Hatherleigh Press is committed to preserving and protecting the natural resources of the Earth. Environmentally responsible and sustainable practices are embraced within the company's mission statement.

Hatherleigh Press is a member of the Publishers Earth Alliance, committed to preserving and protecting the natural resources of the planet while developing a sustainable business model for the book publishing industry.

This book was edited in the village of Hobart, New York. Hobart is a community that has embraced books and publishing as a component of its livelihood. There are several unique bookstores in the village. For more information, please visit www.hobartbookvillage.com.

Library of Congress Cataloging-in-Publication Data
Montgomery, Lisa.
 Raw potluck : over 100 simply delicious raw dishes for everyday entertaining / Lisa Montgomery.
    p. cm. — (Complete book of raw food series)
 ISBN 978-1-57826-398-1 (pbk.)
 1. Raw foods. 2. Raw food diet—Recipes. I. Title. II. Title: Over 100 simply delicious raw dishes for everyday entertaining.
 TX392.M75 2011
 641.5'636—dc23

                        2011031953

Raw Potluck is available for bulk purchase, special promotions, and premiums. For information on reselling and special purchase opportunities, call 1-800-528-2550 and ask for the Special Sales Manager.

Cover design by DCDesign
Interior design by DCDesign

10 9 8 7 6 5 4 3 2 1

Printed in the United States

Some people think that wealth and success are what really matter, but without love, everything else becomes hollow and meaningless. When you love, the rest just comes to you and is put in its proper place.

Thank you to all who have lovingly shared your recipes in Raw Potluck. *Thank you to my readers, who I hope will lovingly make these recipes for yourself and your loved ones.*

> *Many thanks.*
> *Love,*
> *Lisa*

CONTENTS

INTRODUCTION

I was certified as an associate raw chef instructor in July, 2006, at the Living Light Culinary Institute of Raw Foods. Before becoming certified, I had been living a predominantly raw lifestyle, but I decided to go to school to educate myself. I felt that I would eventually be divinely led to where I should go from there, and it did not take long for me to figure out what my next steps would be after my schooling.

While on the plane flying home from school, I was reading a raw resource book that I had picked up, because I wanted more support and, frankly, more raw entertainment than my area was offering at the time. Back then, we only had one monthly raw potluck at a local raw restaurant/store in southeastern Pennsylvania (Arnold's Way in Lansdale, PA). My raw resource book included a section on raw potlucks, so when I got home, I called every raw potluck that was listed in my area. Much to my dismay, every single potluck listed in the book was no longer in existence. Not being a person to wait for someone else to do something for me, I started asking several of my friends if they would attend a monthly raw potluck party if I organized it. They told their friends, who told their friends, who told their friends, and the rest is history.

Now, I hold raw potlucks (a.k.a. parties) regularly. We have had great food every month, and it just keeps getting better. In my newsletter, I share recipes from some of my participating potluckers. In fact, you will find many of those recipes in this book. We have been blessed to have phenomenal local and world-renowned speakers such as Viktoras Kulvinskas, the "grandfather of raw

A spread of delicious dishes from one of Lisa's raw potlucks.

foods." Victoria Boutenko and her daughter, Valya, are two more of our amazing speakers, along with Dr. Roe Gallo, Dr. Doug Graham, Matthew Kenney, Raw Chef Dan, Tonya Zavasta, Matt Monarch, and Brian Clement. We have taken field trips to heirloom organic gardens and fig farms, and we have had wellness expos with guest speakers such as Carol Alt. When I first began throwing these monthly "healthy parties," I never would have guessed that they would grow into such amazing events. In fact, the potlucks have grown so much that I moved them out of my home and into Waterloo Gardens in Exton, PA.

The potluckers are a group of people who share, care, and support each other. Through the potlucks, we have created our own community. So to those who say that one person can't make a difference, I say they can—and I know from experience. Just like they say, "If you build it, they will come," I have learned that if you have a raw potluck, many will come.

Another neat thing about these raw potlucks is that they have gone global thanks to the Internet. I now have people contacting me from all over the world. Plus, I have run into potluckers or folks from the raw community in other states, and I have always been welcomed with a warm hello and hug. I think that we can all use a warm hello and hug, don't you?

With everyone working longer hours than ever before, it is easy to become disconnected. Frankly, most of us do not even know our own neighbors these days. Yet in creating the raw potlucks, I have created a community, and we have had numerous spin-offs. Attendees who have come a long distance or even those who have come a short distance have started their own raw potlucks to support themselves and their community. I have had people come to my potlucks from seven different states. When we first started, I had sixty-five people in my garage, but I have now moved them to Waterloo Gardens because the parties have become so large. People have been blown away that we have gotten so many people to attend when

Sherry Stein's Christmas tree display made of various fruits, including apples, grapes, and kiwis. (Photo courtesy of Sherry Stein)

Linda Louise's Purple and Yellow Eggs (page 95). (Photo courtesy of Linda Cooper).

I am simply opening my house, as opposed to being affiliated with a store or a restaurant.

Raw potlucks can fill in the gaps of our disjointed communities. If you have something that people want to participate in, they will come. The potluckers are an amazing group of intelligent and informed people, and we are never without stimulating conversations. So if you want to have your own raw potluck, try some of the recipes in this book and invite your friends and neighbors. I promise that you all will have a wonderful time (but don't forget to invite me).

Thank you to my potluckers and guest speakers for blessing and enriching my life. Also, many thanks to all of you who have participated in my raw potluck parties, as well as this book.

Thank you,
Lisa

Lisa and Raw Chef Dan

STARTING YOUR OWN RAW POTLUCK

If you want to start your own potluck in your community, start by making a list of all your friends and relatives who you would like to invite. I know that some of the people who came to my first potluck were just coming because they thought I was having a party, and really were not coming because it was going to be a raw potluck. So don't be afraid to invite people who do not typically follow a raw diet.

Here are some other ways to gather people for your potluck:

- When you send out invitations (whether via e-mail, paper, or verbally), ask people to invite their friends or anyone who they think might enjoy the raw potluck, as well.

- Go to your local health store and markets to ask if they will put a blurb on their website, newsletter, and/or bulletin board about your raw potlucks.

- If you are as lucky as I am to have several raw restaurants near you, ask the owners to let everyone know that you will be having a raw potluck.

Once you have invited your people, there are certain things that I have learned through the years:

- Make sure everyone e-mails or brings along a copy of their recipe, since some people may have food allergies and will need to know what each dish contains.

- I typically request that people bring their own dishes. I do provide disposable dishes, but if the potluckers bring their own dishes, it will save on expenses for the hostess, and will also lessen the amount of garbage that will end up in a landfill.

- It can be a lot of fun to have everyone share with the group why they decided to come to the potluck, where they are in their journey, or if they have a business that they want to network.

- After each potluck, I like to send out a newsletter with pictures of the dishes, recipes that were provided by the potluckers, upcoming scheduled events, etc.

- At some of my potlucks, we have had world-renowned speakers: some are local speakers and/or our own potluckers, and other times, it is just us sharing and caring. We have been blessed to have an amazing group of people who are all very talented and knowledgeable.

LIQUID RAW, REVISITED

In my book *Liquid Raw*, I gathered a wide variety of raw smoothies, milks, nogs, soups, and other liquid recipes for you and your family to enjoy. Sharing your favorite "liquid raw" recipes with potluckers and party guests is a great way of introducing the guests to healthy eating or, in this case, drinking. Remember: don't tell your guests that what you are serving is good for them.

Orange/Mango Drink

Dr. Douglas Graham, Food N Sport (www.foodnsport.com), creator of Simply Delicious Cuisine and author of The 80/10/10 Diet

This recipe is inspired by Dr. Doug's book The 80/10/10 Diet.

Prep: 15 minutes

Mango, peeled and pitted
Oranges, peeled

Blend equal quantities of mango and oranges in your Vitamix® and drink. By itself, this is a wonderful drink. As a variation, you can try adding small quantities of any one of the following: strawberry, blueberry, raspberry (or any other berry), pineapple, kiwi (or juice of any other citrus), fennel, basil, dill, any type of mint, vanilla, cinnamon, or raw carob powder.

Dr. Doug is purposefully inexact about his measurement because he likes creations to be up to the creator, rather than being dictated by Dr. Doug. The dishes work equally well whether they are light or heavy in the ingredients.

SJ Energy Special Juice

Sarah-Jayne Bullock, intuitive health and well-being practitioner, focusing on helping people achieve total balance in body, mind, spirit, and life

Towcester, Northamptonshire, UK (www.authentichealthin.com)

Prep: 15 minutes

1 small apple
2 carrots
½ un-waxed lemon
Large handful kale
1 stalk celery
1-inch piece ginger
1 banana
2 handfuls of spinach
1 teaspoon maca powder
1 teaspoon mesquite powder

Juice the first six ingredients in juicer and pour into Vitamix® blender, then blend with the remaining ingredients.

Grafton Lodge Smoothie

Sarah-Jayne Bullock, intuitive health and well-being practitioner, focusing on helping people achieve total balance in body, mind, spirit, and life

Towcester, Northamptonshire, UK (www.authentichealthin.com)

Prep: 15 minutes

1 banana
2 oranges, juiced
½ cup raw coconut meat
2 cups almond milk
Handful spinach

Blend all ingredients together in a Vitamix® blender.

Raw Cacao Beauty Elixir

Potlucker Janice Innella, The Beauty Chef, Philadelphia, PA

Prep: 30 minutes

2 cups almond milk
2 cups coconut water
4 tablespoons raw cacao powder
2 tablespoons raw cacao nibs, for garnish
4 tablespoons hemp seeds
1 tablespoon heaping of coconut oil
1 teaspoon lacuma superfood powder
1 teaspoon blue-green algae powder or 2 capsules
1 teaspoon mesquite superfood powder
1 teaspoon agave inulin powder
4 ounces soaked chia seeds
3 tablespoons fresh chocolate mint leaves
1 teaspoon bee pollen
1 teaspoon probiotic powder or 1 capsule
1 vanilla bean, split in half and scraped out on both sides
Pinch Himalayan sea salt
3 droppers liquid stevia

Combine all of the ingredients together in a Vitamix® until smooth. Chill for an hour and serve in pretty cocktail glasses, garnished with mint and a sprinkling of raw cacao nibs.

Going Green Smoothie

Reproduced and reprinted with the permission of Vitamix® Corporation (www.vitamix.com)

Prep: 10 minutes
Yield: 3½ cups

1 cup green grapes
½ cup pineapple
2 cups fresh spinach
½ ripe banana, peeled
½ cup water
1 cup ice cubes

Place all ingredients into the Vitamix® container in the order listed and secure lid. Select Variable 1. Turn machine on and quickly increase speed to Variable 10, then to High. Blend for 60 seconds or until desired consistency is reached. Serve immediately.

Just Dew It Smoothie

Reproduced and reprinted with the permission of Vitamix® Corporation (www.vitamix.com)

Prep: 5 minutes
Yield: 3¾ cups

¼ cup water
1 cup honeydew, diced
1 medium orange, peeled and halved
½ medium peach, halved and pitted
½ cup pineapple chunks
1 cup ice cubes

Place all ingredients into the Vitamix® container in the order listed and secure lid. Select speed Variable 1. Turn machine on and quickly increase speed to Variable 10, then to High. Blend for 45 seconds or until desired consistency is reached.

Hemp Heaven

Anjou and Jaime Jones, The Date People, (datepeople@wgn.net), California

I buy my dates from Anjou and Jamie, The Date People, who are date farmers in California.

Prep: 5 minutes

½ cup soft dates, pitted
½ cup hemp seeds
4 cups water

Place ingredients in Vitamix® and blend until smooth.

As a variation, try adding your favorite fresh fruit, cacao, vanilla bean, or ice.

Honey Lemonade

Adagio, aged 6, daughter of Jinjee (www.TheGardenDiet.com), created this recipe.

This recipe proves that you are never too young or too old to create amazing raw recipes.

Prep: 10 minutes

3 lemons, juiced
2 tablespoons raw honey
½ blender of water (3 cups)

Blend lemons and honey on high for 30 seconds. Top off blender with water, pour into pitcher, and serve.

Honey Lemonade with Coconut Water

Adagio, aged 6, daughter of Jinjee (www.TheGardenDiet.com)

Prep: 10 minutes

Water of 1 coconut
½ pitcher Honey Lemonade (see page xx)

Combine all ingredients and serve.

Kale and Pear Green Smoothie

Reproduced and reprinted with the permission of Vitamix® Corporation (www.vitamix.com)

Prep: 10 minutes
Yield: 4 cups

1 cup green grapes
1 orange, peeled
½ Bartlett pear
1 banana, fresh or frozen, peeled
1 cup kale
½ cup water
2 cups ice cubes

Place all ingredients into the Vitamix® container in the order listed and secure lid. Select Variable 1. Turn machine on and quickly increase speed to Variable 10, then to High. Blend for 1½ minutes or until desired consistency is reached.

Raw Sesame Power Drink

Potlucker Dawn Light, author of Dawn of a New Day Raw Desserts, *Phoenixville, PA. Dawn also reviews books and products that support Lifestyles of Health and Sustainability (LOHAS) at www.dawnofanewday.com.*

Prep: 15 minutes

1 cup sesame seeds
3–4 cups filtered water
Raw honey or raw coconut crystals, to taste
1 teaspoon maca powder
1 teaspoon mesquite powder
1 tablespoon chia or Salba® seeds per serving

Grind sesame seeds in a blender or coffee grinder. Grind until seeds are milled, but not congealed (if using a coffee grinder, put the ground sesame seeds into a blender).

Add 3–4 cups water and sesame seeds to the blender and blend for 30 seconds. Strain through a fine mesh "nut milk" bag (I like to use a nut milk bag with a drawstring). Close the drawstring and set it in a strainer that is on top of a deep bowl (which it fits onto perfectly), and then let it strain out of the bag until it is almost done. Then squeeze the rest of the nut milk out of the sesame pulp.

Return the sesame milk to the blender with remaining ingredients (except chia or Salba® seeds). Blend until mixed well. Pour into glasses, add 1 tablespoon chia or Salba® seeds, and stir well. Continue to stir the seeds around so they do not congeal at the bottom of your glass. After 15 minutes, the seeds are considered sprouted, and you have a yummy power drink. Store unused drink in the refrigerator.

Realitini

Rose Realitini

Prep: 10 minutes

3 limes, juiced
1 quart water
1 tablespoon Simply SBGA (powdered algae from Simplexity®)
2 teaspoons rose water
1 cup ice
½ cup sweetener like raw honey or agave, to taste.

Blend the ingredients together in a Vitamix®. Blend and serve in martini glasses.

Tao de Ching

Katherine Clark (Healthworkshi@gmail.com, www.kclark.biz)

Prep: 5 minutes

Oranges, juiced
1 teaspoon Simply SBGA (powdered algae from Simplexity®)

Pour fresh orange juice into glasses and stir in 1 teaspoon of Simply SBGA. Can be served in 2-ounce shot glasses.

Wheat Grass Cocktail

Reproduced and reprinted with the permission of Vitamix® Corporation (www.vitamix.com)

Prep: 10 minutes
Yield: 2 cups

½ cup water
1 cup grapes
½ cup pineapple
½ cup wheat grass
1 cup ice cubes

Place all ingredients into the Vitamix® container in the order listed and secure lid. Select Variable 1. Turn machine on and quickly increase speed to Variable 10, then to High. Blend for 1 minute or until desired consistency is reached.

Lisa's "No More Coconuts" Smoothie

Lisa Montgomery

Prep: 10 minutes

3 bananas (fresh or frozen)
1 tray ice cubes
1 cup strawberries (fresh or frozen)
8 ounces water
3 dates, pitted
1 orange, peeled

Combine the above ingredients together in a Vitamix®. Blend until smooth.

You may be asking why I called this the "No More Coconuts" Smoothie. I have been using young Thai coconuts as one of the bases for my smoothies for years. Recently, their cost increased greatly at the Asian markets, and they are now unavailable at most health stores. No one has any idea why they have become unavailable or when they will be stocked again. There is good news, though: believe it or not, big box grocery stores are now carrying young Thai coconuts. Nonetheless, if you are still having trouble finding coconuts in your area, you can turn to this recipe as an alternative.

Spicy Pineapple Crush

Brenda Cobb, founder of Living Foods Institute in Atlanta, GA (www.livingfoodsinstitute.com) and author of The Living Foods Lifestyle

Prep: 10 minutes

3 cups very ripe, fresh pineapple
2 teaspoons mint leaves
1 teaspoon cilantro
1 teaspoon fresh lemon juice
Pinch cayenne pepper

Blend ingredients together in the Vitamix®. Serve and refresh yourself.

Pumpkin Seeds Orange Drink

Austria's Finest, Naturally, Helco Ltd., Mt. Vernon, VA (www.austrianpumpkinoil.com)

Prep: 5 minutes

1 cup orange juice
3 teaspoons ground pumpkin seeds
1 teaspoon raw honey

Blend all the ingredients together well.

Pumpkin Seed Tomato Drink

Austria's Finest, Naturally, Helco Ltd., Mt. Vernon, VA
(www.austrianpumpkinoil.com)

Prep: 10 minutes

2 cups tomato juice
2 teaspoons ground pumpkin seeds
1 cup water
1 teaspoon fresh mixed herbs
Salt, to taste

Blend all the ingredients together well.

Mediterranean Soup

Victoria Boutenko, The Raw Family, author of many books such as
Green for Life *and* The 12 Steps to Raw Food

Prep: 10 minutes
Yield: 8 cups

2 cups filtered water
3 stalks celery, quartered
1 sprig oregano
1 sprig thyme
1 red bell pepper, seeded and stemmed, cut into chunks
1 avocado, pitted and peeled
1 cucumber, cut into chunks
1 jalapeño
1 lime, peeled, halved, and seeded
3 cups spinach

Place all ingredients, except spinach, into the Vitamix® container in the order listed and secure lid. Select speed Variable 1. Turn machine on and quickly increase speed to Variable 10, then to High. Blend for 10 seconds, using the tamper to press the ingredients into the blades. Once the mixture begins to circulate and head room is created at the top of the machine, stop machine and remove lid. Add spinach leaves and secure lid. Continue blending on High speed for 30 seconds. Enjoy with dulse leaves or flakes. This recipe can be reduced by half and made in smaller containers.

Savory Basil Soup

Victoria Boutenko, The Raw Family, author of many books such as Green for Life *and* The 12 Steps to Raw Food

Prep: 10 minutes
Yield: 4 cups

1 cup filtered water
1 bunch fresh basil
2 large, ripe tomatoes, quartered
1 bell pepper, seeded and stemmed
2 garlic cloves, peeled
3 cups Savoy cabbage, chopped
3 sliced green onions
½ cup dulse leaves
½ avocado, cubed

Place the water, basil, tomatoes, bell pepper, and garlic into the Vitamix® container in the order listed and secure lid. Select speed Variable 1. Turn machine on and quickly increase speed to Variable 10, then to High. Blend for 30–45 seconds, using the tamper to press the ingredients into the blades. Pour into the large bowl. Add remaining ingredients.

Coconut Honey Cream

Potlucker Dawn Light, author of Dawn of a New Day Raw Desserts, *Phoenixville, PA. Dawn also reviews books and products that support Lifestyles of Health and Sustainability (LOHAS) at www.dawnofanewday.com.*

Prep: 10 minutes

1 cup raw coconut butter
1 cup raw honey

Place coconut butter in a bowl, and beat with beaters until it is creamy and all lumps are gone. Add honey and continue to beat until well-mixed and creamy.

Coconut butter has a low melting point so make sure that you purchase coconut butter, not coconut oil, for this recipe. Once the recipe is done, it will need to be kept below the melting point or it will separate. Raw honey solidifies, but it can be used in this recipe either as a solid or liquid.

Coconut Honey Cream is great served on your favorite raw cookies or crackers. It is very sweet so a little goes a long way.

Raw Non-Dairy Blueberry "Yogurt"

Rhonda Malkmus, Hallelujah Acres (www.hacres.com), Shelby, NC

Prep: 10 minutes

1 cup blueberries
1 medium-sized avocado
2 Medjool dates, pitted
Water, enough for desired consistency

Set aside ⅛ cup of the blueberries. Then place the remaining blueberries, along with the other ingredients, in a Vitamix® and blend, adding enough distilled water to obtain desired consistency. Remove from the blender and stir in the whole blueberries that were set aside earlier.

If you desire a sweeter-tasting yogurt, you can add a teaspoon (or to taste) of agave nectar. A few drops of vanilla extract also add a lot of flavor. If you want a livelier, friendlier bacteria, you can open a probiotic capsule and add its contents to the yogurt.

You could also use strawberries or raspberries.

Creamy Cucumber Dill Dressing

Karen Ranzi, author of Creating Healthy Children

Prep: 7 minutes
Soak: dates, ½ hour

2 tablespoons pine nuts
1½ cups cucumbers, peeled and chopped
2 stalks celery
2 dates, pitted and soaked for ½ hour if not soft
½ lemon, juiced
½ cup fresh dill, chopped

Blend all ingredients together in a Vitamix® and pour onto leafy green salad.

Toasted Sesame Mayo
Lisa Montgomery

Prep: 7 minutes

1 cup raw cashews
½ cup water
½ teaspoon sea salt
1 teaspoon lemon juice
½ teaspoon agave
½ teaspoon toasted sesame oil
1 teaspoon black sesame seeds

Combine all ingredients (except black sesame seeds) in a Vitamix® high-speed blender until creamy-smooth. Pour mayo mixture into a bowl and manually stir in the black sesame seeds with a spoon.

This is to die for. I absolutely love it. You can use it as a dip, dressing, or as a replacement for tartar sauce or regular mayonnaise when making veggie or un-crab burgers. This is also great when making a collard wrap, which you fill with julienned vegetables, and use this as a dip on the inside of the wrap as well as the outside. I hope you like this as much as I do.

How long does it last? I don't know; I always eat it before it has a chance to spoil.

Tomato Sauce

Dr. Roe Gallo, author of Overcoming the Myths of Aging

Prep: 10 minutes

1 cup sun-dried tomatoes
1 cup fresh tomatoes
½ red pepper
1 whole scallion
2 teaspoons olive oil
Fresh basil, to taste

Chop sun-dried tomatoes, fresh tomatoes, red peppers, scallion, and basil in a food processor. Add olive oil and serve.

> You can make this sauce chunky or smooth, and/or change the ratio of the ingredients, depending on the taste you want to achieve.

Cranberry Sauce

Dr. Roe Gallo, author of Overcoming the Myths of Aging

Prep: 7 minutes

1 pound fresh cranberries
1 tablespoon fresh mint
⅓ cup agave (more or less to taste)

In the food processor, chop cranberries and mint together using a pulsing action to leave coarsely chopped. Add agave to taste.

This can be served alone or over a bed of lettuce.

Autumn Gold Soup

Rhonda Malkmus, Hallelujah Acres (www.hacres.com), Shelby, NC

Prep: 20 minutes
Serves: 3

3 cups distilled water, warmed, but not boiling
2½ cups carrot pieces
1 yellow or orange bell pepper, seeded
1 small green onion, quartered
3 tablespoons raw almond butter
½ clove garlic
¼ teaspoon cayenne pepper
1 teaspoon garam masala
½ teaspoon cinnamon powder
1½ Celtic sea salt (optional)
2 tablespoons apple cider vinegar

Blend all of the above ingredients together in a Vitamix® until smooth. Garnish with shredded cucumber or mint leaves and a few drops of olive oil.

Tomato Mango Soup

Dr. Douglas Graham, Food N Sport (www.foodnsport.com), creator of Simply Delicious Cuisine and author of The 80/10/10 Diet

Prep: 10 minutes

Tomato
Mango, peeled and pitted

Combine equal parts tomatoes and mangos in a food processor, creating a chunky mixture.

Optional: Serve over a bed of "rice" made from chopped chayote, jicama, mung bean sprouts, white cabbage, cauliflower, or any other white and suitably coarse vegetable.

Creamy Sweet Balsamic

Sheryll Chavarria, Raw Can Roll Café and Pure Body Spa,
Douglassville, PA (www.rawcanrollcafe.com)

Prep: 10 minutes

¼-½ cup olive oil
¾ cup water
1 cup balsamic vinegar
3 or 4 cloves garlic
1 tablespoon sea salt
4 tablespoons agave
2 handfuls basil
1 avocado

Place all ingredients together in a Vitamix® and blend until creamy.

FINGER FUN FOOD

I absolutely adore fun finger foods. I have been known to have dinner parties where the entire meal is finger food. Plus, I must confess that I cannot eat that much, and I always seem to be on the go so finger food is great for every day living, as well as entertaining. It is much easier for a guest to enjoy chatting and still be able to eat finger food versus a sit-down meal.

Rustic Tomato Bread

Alorah Arliotis (www.thewiserwoman.co.uk), Glastonbury, England

Alorah holds sacred retreats in Corfu and Glastonbury to help people find spiritual guidance. Check out her website for more information.

Prep: 30 minutes
Dehydrate: 7 hours at 115°F

1 cup whole flax seeds, ground
½ cup whole flax, left whole
¼ cup pumpkin seeds, ground
½ tablespoon dried oregano
1 tablespoon dried basil
½ teaspoon cayenne pepper
4 pounds (2 kilograms) Roma tomatoes, chopped to very
      fine pieces
¼ cup cold-pressed olive oil
2 teaspoons nama shoyu

Place all dry ingredients into a large bowl and mix with a spoon or by hand. Add finely chopped tomatoes and mix well. Add the remaining ingredients and mix well. Spread mixture onto Teflex sheets of your dehydrator, and score into desired shapes and sizes. Dehydrate for 7 hours at 115°F. If breads are too moist, dehydrate until desired consistency. Halfway through dehydrating, flip the crackers and remove the Teflex sheets.

Kale Cheese Chips

Potlucker Vito Natalie, photographer, video-photographer, musician, and raw chef

Prep: 20 minutes
Soak: cashews, 1 hour
Dehydrate: 12½ hours at 105°F

2 cups raw cashews, soaked

3 tablespoons nutritional yeast

2 basil leaves, chopped

1 tablespoon parsley, chopped

3 tablespoons Bragg® Apple Cider Vinegar

1 tablespoon Bragg® Liquid Aminos

1 clove garlic, minced

All-natural onion, oregano, and herbs

1 tablespoon light agave nectar

½ cup sunflower seeds

2 cups water, as needed

1 large lemon, juiced

2 bunches of kale, stems removed

Sea salt, to taste

Mix the above ingredients together in a Vitamix® except for the kale. Place kale in large bowl, pour the liquid, blended mixture over the kale, and mix with your hands. Dehydrate for 12½ hours at 105°F.

Spinach Basil Pesto

Potluckers Bruce and Marsha Weinstein, Awesome Foods, Bridgeport, PA (www.awesomefoods.com)

Prep: 15 minutes
Soak: walnuts, 4 hours; sunflower seeds, 6 hours

2.2 ounces soaked raw walnuts

2.2 ounces soaked raw sunflower seeds

2.3 ounces cold-pressed olive oil

2 ounces fresh basil (please wash)

2.3 ounces spinach

0.3 ounces fresh garlic

0.6 ounces fresh lemon juice

0.9 ounces water

Pinch dried basil

¼ teaspoon Himalayan sea salt

Combine ingredients in a Vitamix® and blend well.

This pesto can be used as a dip, as a pesto on spiralized pasta, as a dressing on a salad, as a coating for kale chips, as a spread on crackers, or as a pesto on pizza.

Pine Nut-Dill "Cheese" Spread

Elaina Love, author of Pure Joy Kitchen *(www.purejoyplanet.com)*

Prep: 20 minutes

2 cups soaked and peeled (optional) almonds (1½ cups before
     soaking)

¼-½ cup purified water (amount needed may vary)

½ cup pine nuts, chopped

½ cup red onion, minced

2 green onions, minced

2 tablespoons raw, light miso (look for unpasteurized in the
     refrigerator section)

1 tablespoon nutritional yeast (not a raw food)

2 cloves garlic, crushed

4 tablespoons parsley, chopped

2 teaspoons fresh dill, chopped

Peel almonds by soaking in hot water for 20–30 seconds, then draining and removing the skins. The almonds should slide out of the skins with this method. This is optional for a lighter textured paste.

Run almonds through the juicer using the blank blade or put in food processor. Alternate water with nuts to keep them moving through the machine. If using a food processor, add water after the nuts are pureed well. Add remainder of ingredients and mix well. Form into a round or square shape. Garnish with a sprig of dill or parsley and chopped dehydrated almonds. Serve with fresh vegetables or flax crackers. Makes 3 cups.

Living, Dehydrated Herb Flax Crackers

Elaina Love, author of Pure Joy Kitchen *(www.purejoyplanet.com)*

Prep: 20 minutes
Soak: flax seeds, 24 hours
Dehydrate: about 24 hours at 105°F

½ onion

5 cloves garlic

4 cups flax seeds, soaked (seeds will double in size so put them in an 8-cup container, fill to the top with water, and then store in a dark place)

2 teaspoons sea salt

¼ cup lemon juice

1 cup chopped fresh dill, and/or rosemary, sage, basil, oregano, thyme, cilantro

Puree onions, garlic, and herbs in a food processor until finely ground. In a large bowl, combine sprouted flax seeds, salt, lemon juice, and herb mixture. Place 2 cups in the middle of a Teflex dehydrator sheet using a plastic spatula. Take the corner edge of your firm spatula and score the sheets into 25 squares. You should fill 4 16x16-inch trays. The thicker you make them, the easier they are to dip with. Dehydrate at 105°F until crackers are firm enough to flip. Let crackers remain in dehydrator until crunchy (about 24 hours all together). Makes approximately 100 crackers.

Garlic Bread

Elaina Love, author of Pure Joy Kitchen *(www.purejoyplanet.com)*

Prep: 30 minutes
Dehydrate: 6–8 hours at 105°F

6 cups almond meal (leftover from making almond milk)
2 cups flax meal (1¼ cups flax seeds ground in a dry blender)
½ cup Bariani® Olive Oil
2 teaspoons Celtic sea salt
2–3 crushed garlic cloves
½ cup chopped fresh Italian herbs: basil, oregano, thyme, and
         rosemary
Pitted and sliced sun-dried olives, optional

Place all ingredients in a bowl and mix with your hands. Place some of the batter in between 2 Teflex sheets or wax paper, and roll with a rolling pin until the batter is about ¼-inch thick. Cut into bread-sized pieces or use fun cookie cutter shapes.

Dehydrate at 105°F for 6 to 8 hours. Bread should be moist and firm. You can also sun-dry these on a screen or put them in your car to dry on a warm day. Will last 2 weeks in the refrigerator.

Twice-Soaked Bread

Potlucker Alan Ritter

Prep: 40 minutes
Soak: flax seeds and buckwheat groats, 12 hours

Pear Puree
2 cups ripened pears
1 tablespoon cinnamon (or to taste)

Sprout Mix
1 pound bananas, peeled
2 cups water plus small amount to keep sprout mix pliable
2 cups flax seed
2 cups buckwheat groats

Apple Dice
10 cups Granny Smith apples, diced, peeled, and cored

Pear Puree
Puree pears and cinnamon together. This will make 2 cups of pear puree.

Sprout Mix
Blend bananas and 2 cups of water to form a banana puree. Use the banana puree to soak the flax seeds and buckwheat groats for 12 hours. After the initial banana puree and during the 12 hours, add a small amount of water to sprouting mixture to prevent from becoming too dry. The final sprouted mix will have a hard, but pliable consistency. There will be no standing water. This makes about 9 cups.

This is the first flavor-adding "soak."

Apple Dice
Medium dice 10 cups of Granny Smith apples.

Assembly
In a food processor, add half of the soaked sprout mix and 1 cup of pear puree. Combine, but do not over-process and fully break down the sprouts. You may need to add a small amount of water depending on your conditions.

In a bowl, fold 5 cups (half) of the diced apples into this processed mixture and lay this mixture out on 2 dehydrator sheets (half on each). The height of the apple dice will require 2 bays in your dehydrator.

Repeat the steps with the other half of the total recipe to fill a total of 4 dehydrator sheets in a 9-bay dehydrator. The entire machine is filled due to the extra height requirement of the granola bar.

Spread mixture on Teflex sheets and place in dehydrator at 105°F until desired doneness. Flip crackers halfway through the dehydration process. Makes 4 dehydrator sheets of "granola bar."

Stuffed Tomatoes

Sheryll Chavarria, Raw Can Roll Café and Pure Body Spa,
Douglassville, PA (www.rawcanrollcafe.com)

Prep: 15 minutes

Guacamole/Avocado Filling
4–6 avocados, coarsely mashed
2 cloves garlic, minced
1 bunch cilantro, finely chopped
1 large tomato, chopped
1 onion, finely chopped
1 jalapeño pepper (optional)
2 limes or lemons, juiced (optional)
Sea salt, to taste

Tomato Shell
4 large tomatoes

Guacamole/Avocado Filling
Mix all ingredients together in a mixing bowl.

Assembly
Cut a slice from the bottom of the tomato. Remove the insides of the tomato with a spoon. Be careful not to puncture the walls of the tomato. Fill tomato with guacamole-avocado filling and serve.

Blueberry Muffins

Rhio, author of Hooked on Raw

Prep: 30 minutes
Soak: barley, 24 hours; Brazil nuts, 8 hours or overnight;
Hunza raisins, 1 hour
Dehydrate: 24 hours at 100°F

2 cups soaked and/or sprouted barley

1½ cups Brazil nuts, soaked and drained

¼ cup golden flax seed, ground

2 fresh dates (or 4 dried, soaked 1 hour)

2 cups Hunza raisins, soaked and strained (this will swell so you
   will have more than 2 cups)

2–4 tablespoon raw honey

1 tablespoon extra-virgin olive oil

2 teaspoons cinnamon

½ vanilla bean, ground (approximately ½ teaspoon)

¾–1 cup blueberries

Place the first 3 ingredients into a food processor with the "S" blade and blend as finely as possible. You might have to do this in batches depending on the size of your food processor. Transfer mixture to a large mixing bowl.

Place dates, 2 cups of the raisins, honey, olive oil, cinnamon, and vanilla bean into the food processor, and blend very well using the "S" blade. Add mixture to the bowl. Also, add in ½ cup of soaked raisins and mix everything very well by hand.

Place the blueberries into the food processor utilizing the "S" blade. Pulse-chop to break up the blueberries a little bit, and then add blueberries to the ingredients in the bowl and mix well.

. . . *continued on next page*

Form into round, flat muffins approximately ½-inch high and 2–2½-inches in diameter.

Place on Teflex-lined trays and dehydrate at 100°F for 24 hours or until resembling muffin consistency. Halfway through, turn the muffins over on the mesh screen (removing Teflex sheet) and finish dehydrating.

When soaking the barley, be sure to change the water twice during the 24 hours. If you want to sprout the barley as well, allow it to sprout for a few days after soaking and be sure to rinse twice each day.

Sunflower Dill Wafers

Potlucker Janice Innella, The Beauty Chef, Philadelphia, PA

Prep: 25 minutes
Soak: sunflower seeds, 4 hours
Dehydrate: 14 hours at 115°F

1½ cups golden flax seed, ground up in coffee grinder
2 cups pure water
4 cups sunflower seeds, soaked, drained, and rinsed
1 cup fresh dill
2 cups green zucchini
1 medium-sized red onion
1 tablespoon Himalayan sea salt
2 tablespoons caraway seeds, ground
2 ounces cold-pressed olive oil

Combine flax seeds and water in a large bowl. In a food processor, grind up your sunflower seeds so they are still chunky. Add processed sunflower seeds to the mixture in a large bowl. Place dill, zucchini, and onion in your food process and grind until smooth. Remove from the food processor and add to the mixture in the bowl along with salt and caraway seeds. Add the olive oil to the cracker batter once all ingredients are ground and put into a large bowl, then hand-mix all ingredients together.

On a Teflex sheet, place 12 ounces of cracker batter, smooth out to the edges, and pre-score in small squares. This will make 4 trays. Dehydrate at 115°F for 8 hours. Flip and dry for another 6 hours. Store in an air-tight, dry container. Serve with any dip.

To pre-score the batter, use a knife or pizza cutter to score the dough into whichever cracker shape you would like. This will show you where to break the cracker apart when it dries.

Stuffed Mushrooms

Potlucker Jean Cuce

Jean is a CFO for a consulting firm, owns a tax practice, and also owns Victoria Natural Farm with her husband, Aldo. Victoria Natural Farm is located in Worcester Township, PA, and specializes in several Italian fig trees, producing fresh figs, local honey, and organic produce. I held my June, 2011, raw potluck at Jean's Victoria Natural Farm. Jean grows all the herbs Victoria Natural Farm produces. Visit Jean on Facebook by searching for "Jean Marie Cuce."

Prep: 25 minutes
Soak: walnuts, 6 hours

16 mushrooms of your choice, cleaned and dried
Bragg® Liquid Aminos, enough to cover mushrooms while
    marinating
2 cups red bell pepper, chopped
1½ cups raw walnuts, soaked and dehydrated
1 cup carrot, chopped
1 cup red onion, chopped
⅔ cup fresh basil, chopped
20 sun-dried black olives, pitted
2 cloves garlic
2 teaspoons dried oregano

Clean mushrooms and marinate in Bragg® Liquid Aminos for 30 minutes prior to stuffing.

In a food processor, combine the remaining ingredients and process to form a pate consistency. Season to taste. Use this mixture to fill the mushrooms. Let stand for 30 minutes.

Serve immediately or dehydrate overnight, and then serve.

Jean brought this dish to my December, 2010, raw potluck. When she walked through the front door, the aroma was heavenly, and I could not wait until dinner. The advantage of being the hostess is I get to sneak a taste, and they were as good as they looked and smelled. This recipe was the hit of the potluck.

Sunny Crisps

Brenda Cobb, founder of Living Foods Institute in Atlanta, GA (www.livingfoodsinstitute.com) and author of The Living Foods Lifestyle

Prep: 20 minutes
Soak: sunflower seeds, almonds, and flax seeds, overnight
Dehydrate: 1–2 days at 100°F

1 cup sunflower seeds, soaked

1 cup almonds, soaked

1 cup hemp seeds

1 cup flax seeds, soaked

7 cups water

¼ teaspoon cayenne pepper

2 cups carrots

1 tablespoon cumin powder

2 teaspoon Himalayan sea salt

3 cups fresh tomatoes

1 cup onion

Soak the sunflower seeds, almonds, hemp, and flax seeds in 7 cups of water overnight and drain. Place the cayenne pepper, carrots, cumin, salt, tomato, and onion in the food processor, and blend until creamy. Add the seeds and nuts, and continue blending until all the ingredients are mixed together well and the nuts are finely chopped (you want the batter to be creamy and easy to spread).

Spread the mixture on Teflex dehydrator sheets and dehydrate overnight at 100°F. Flip the crackers and continue dehydrating another day until crispy.

Pesto Spinach Portobello

Brenda Cobb, founder of Living Foods Institute in Atlanta, GA (www.livingfoodsinstitute.com) and author of The Living Foods Lifestyle

Prep: 30 minutes
Soak: walnuts and sunflower seeds, overnight

1 cup walnuts, soaked and drained
1 cup sunflower seeds, soaked and drained
24 small Portobello mushroom caps
½ cup plus 1 tablespoon nama shoyu raw soy sauce
½ cup fresh lemon juice
2 tablespoons fresh ginger, chopped
½ cup water
2 tablespoons garlic
2 teaspoons fresh jalapeño pepper, seeded
4 cups spinach, packed very tightly
½ cup parsley, packed very tightly
½ cup fresh basil
¼ teaspoon psyllium
1 teaspoon Himalayan sea salt
1 red bell pepper, seeded

Soak the walnuts and sunflower seeds in 5 cups of filtered, alkaline water overnight and drain.

Remove the stems from the mushrooms. Combine the ½ cup of nama shoyu, lemon juice, ginger, salt, and water to create a marinade. Marinate the mushrooms overnight. Take the mushrooms out of the marinade and pat dry.

. . . continued on next page

Chop the garlic, jalapeño pepper, spinach, parsley, basil, and 1 tablespoon of nama shoyu in the food processor until well-blended. Add the walnuts, sunflower seeds, and psyllium to the mixture, and continue to blend until creamy and thick.

Fill the mushroom caps with the spinach pesto and decorate with minced red pepper.

Dehydrated Seed Crackers

Potlucker Nancy List, certified teacher of transcendental meditation

Prep: 30 minutes
Soak: sunflower seeds and pumpkin seeds, overnight; golden flax seeds, 2 hours
Dehydrate: 14–18 hours at 105°F

3 cups sunflower seeds, soaked
3 cups pumpkin seeds, soaked
2 cups golden flax seeds, soaked
1 cup sesame seeds, hulled
2 cups celery
2 cups carrots
1 cup fresh parsley
2–3 cloves garlic
Water, enough to blend
1 tablespoon cumin
Bragg® Liquid Aminos, to taste

Rinse the sunflower seeds and pumpkin seeds, and place them in a Vitamix® with just enough water to blend. Add the flax seeds and sesame seeds to batter after you have run the sunflower seeds and pumpkin seeds through the Vitamix®, and blend by hand.

Use a food processor to chop the celery, carrots, parsley, and garlic. Add enough water to blend.

Add the cumin and Bragg® to the food processor mixture. Spread batter on Teflex sheets and dehydrate at 105°F for 8–12 hours. Turn the crackers over, score, remove from the Teflex sheets, and dehydrate for another 6 hours on the rack or until the crackers are dry enough to break apart and store.

Just Above Simple Spaghetti Sauce/ Tomato Soup

Potlucker Alan Ritter

Prep: 15 minutes

7–8 Roma tomatoes
1 red pepper
1 bunch cilantro
1 packet basil (1½ ounces)
3–4 stalks celery
2 dates, pitted
½ avocado
1–2 cloves garlic
2 pinches dried garlic

Blend ingredients together in a Vitamix® high-speed blender. Add tomatoes first. Do not add water.

Simple Bananas with Cinnamon and Curry

Potlucker Alan Ritter

Prep: 5 minutes

4 bananas
Dusting of cinnamon
Dusting of curry

In a bowl, slice bananas and sprinkle with cinnamon and curry powder to taste. The taste accents of the sweet and spicy are yummy.

Garlic Bread

Joel Odhner, Catalyst Cleanse, Rawlife Line, Philadelphia, PA

Prep: 15 minutes
Dehydrate: 4–8 hours at 105°F

Jicama, peeled and sliced ¼-inch thick
1 cup flax seeds, ground
1½ cups walnuts
4 or 5 cloves garlic
1 teaspoon lemon juice
1 teaspoon sea salt (or to taste)

Peel and slice the jicama and lay out on Teflex sheets. Combine the rest of the ingredients in your food processor and hand-press the mixture onto jicama slices. Dehydrate 4–8 hours.

This is one of the first recipes that Joel taught me at his raw cooking classes. This recipe is easy and so good. It is one of those recipes that, once you start eating it, you just keep going. If you would make this recipe as a snack for your family, they will devour it.

SIDES

The great thing about sides is that sometimes they are so great and, depending on how you present them, they can become the "main event." For example, a pâté on a bed of greens and assorted vegetables now becomes the highlight of the meal. Yet that same pâté can be used to stuff celery sticks, act as a spread on crackers, as a snack or an appetizer, or as a dip for crudités. One simple recipe, like a little black dress, is extremely versatile, depending on how you accessorize it.

Un (Shhh) Egg Salad

Lisa Montgomery

Please, please don't tell my chickens that I created an egg-less egg salad. They would not be happy with me if they found out that I was not using their eggs for this salad. So shhh…don't tell.

Prep: 25 minutes

Base
1½ cups cashews
1 cup pine nuts
2–3 cloves garlic
2 heaping teaspoons turmeric
2 tablespoons apple cider vinegar
½ cup lemon juice
2 teaspoons sea salt
1 tablespoon nutritional yeast (optional)
3 tablespoons agave
¾ cup water

Chopped Ingredients
4 tablespoons red onion, chopped
4 tablespoons red pepper, chopped
4 tablespoons olives, chopped
4 tablespoons celery, chopped

Base
Combine all ingredients in a Vitamix® high speed blender until smooth and set aside in a bowl.

Chopped Ingredients
Stir in the chopped onion, pepper, olives, and celery with the base mixture. Serve on a bed of lettuce, on a cracker, or use as a dip.

Pickle and Pimento

Lisa Montgomery

Prep: 25 minutes
Soak: cashews, 4 hours; sunflower seeds, 6 hours; almonds, 8 hours

¼ cup almonds, soaked
½ cup cashews, soaked
¾ cup sunflower seeds, soaked
½ cup water
1 garlic clove, minced
1 tablespoon agave
1 teaspoon lemon juice
½ teaspoon sea salt
1 tablespoon olive oil
¼ cup pimentos, chopped
¼ cup olives, chopped
¼ cup Bubbies® Raw Pickles, chopped (optional)

Combine in a Vitamix® high-speed blender the almonds, cashews, sunflower seeds, water, garlic, agave, lemon juice, salt, and olive oil. You can either blend until creamy or leave chunky. If you wish your pâté to be creamy, you will need to stop and scrape down the sides of the blender several times. You may also have to add more water or olive oil. If you wish the pâté to be chunky like a tuna salad, then blend until chunky, but blended. Set aside

. . . continued on next page

pâté in a bowl. Finely chop pimentos and olives, and stir into the pâté with the raw pickles (optional).

When I came up with this recipe, I knew that I wanted to make a pickle and pimento to replace the pickle and pimento cold-cuts that I used to enjoy when I ate a standard American diet. So when I came up with the recipe, I added in my pimentos and olives, later realizing I had forgotten the pickles. Ironically, I actually preferred it without the pickles. Try it both ways and see what you like the best.

Dr. D's 80/10/10 Salad

Dr. Douglas Graham, Food N Sport (www.foodnsport.com), creator of Simply Delicious Cuisine and author of The 80/10/10 Diet

This recipe was inspired by Dr. Doug's book, The 80/10/10 Diet.

Prep: 20 minutes

Broccoli
Celery
Avocado
Mango, peeled and seeded
Tomato
Fresh cilantro
Chives (optional)
Cucumbers

Combine and chop broccoli, celery, avocado, and mango in your food processor using an "S" blade. Set mixture aside. Finely chop tomatoes, cilantro, and chives (if using). Mix all the ingredients together (except the cucumber). Serve the mixture on top of a bed of sliced cucumbers.

Strawberry Sunflower Coleslaw

Alorah Arliotis (www.thewiserwoman.co.uk), Glastonbury, England

Alorah holds sacred retreats in Corfu and Glastonbury to help people find spiritual guidance. Check out her website for more information.

Prep: 25 minutes
Soak: sunflower seeds and walnuts, 4 hours

⅓ head green cabbage, finely shredded or finely sliced
2 carrots, peeled and grated
2 stalks, celery, diced
1 apple, cored and diced
⅓ cup sunflower seeds, soaked and drained
⅓ cup walnut pieces, soaked, drained, and chopped
10–12 strawberries, sliced

Dressing
¼ cup organic mayonnaise or raw mayonnaise
3 teaspoons wheat-free tamari
1 orange, juiced
1 tablespoon cold-pressed olive oil
Salt and pepper, to taste

Combine all ingredients together in a large mixing bowl, making sure that the cabbage and vegetables are totally covered with the dressing. Chill for at least 20 minutes. Before serving, garnish with a sprinkling of fresh strawberries.

Thai Sprout Salad with Kelp Noodles

Potlucker Janice Innella, The Beauty Chef, Philadelphia, PA

Prep: 30 minuets
Soak and sprout: mung beans, adjuki beans, pea sprouts, and lentils, 5 days

Salad

2 ounces mung beans, soaked and sprouted

2 ounces adjuki beans, soaked and sprouted

2 ounces pea sprouts, soaked and sprouted

2 ounces lentils, soaked and sprouted

1 red pepper, chopped

1 medium red onion, chopped

1 clove garlic, minced

1 bunch fresh cilantro, chopped

1 fennel bulb, chopped

1 (12 ounce) bag raw kelp noodles, rinsed, drained, and chopped

Dressing

½ cup dark sesame oil

2 tablespoons umeboshi plum paste

2 tablespoons ginger, juiced or grated

1 tablespoon nama shoyu

1 teaspoon Thai chili paste or 1 small dry Thai chili

1 medium shallot

. . . continued on next page

Salad

Prep time for sprouts is 5 days: Soak all beans and pea sprouts overnight in a large gallon jar with a screen or piece of cheesecloth on top. Empty water and refill, and then rinse well and empty water, again. Let drain on drain board and sit until the evening. Repeat this process 2–3 times a day for 5 days. Sprouts will be ready for salad when they have long tails.

In a large bowl, add the sprouts, red pepper, red onion, garlic, cilantro, and fennel. Cut up kelp noodles so they are in bite-sized pieces.

Dressing

Combine all ingredients together in a Vitamix® until smooth.

Serve the salad in a large bowl and garnish with cilantro and extra red pepper pieces. Add the dressing as desired. Dressing will last for 2 weeks in a refrigerator.

Delicious Broccoli-Grape Salad

Rhonda Malkmus, Hallelujah Acres (www.hacres.com), Shelby, NC

Prep: 20 minutes

2 heads fresh broccoli, cut into bite-sized florets
½ cup celery, diced finely
½ cup green onion, sliced thinly
1 cup organic seedless, green grapes
1 cup organic seedless red grapes
½ cup organic raisins
½ cup pecan pieces

Place all ingredients in a large bowl and toss well. Add your favorite salad dressing.

South of the Border Slaw

Rhonda Malkmus, Hallelujah Acres (www.hacres.com), Shelby, NC

Prep: 30 minutes

Slaw

3 cups green cabbage, sliced thinly

3 cups red cabbage, sliced thinly

1 large carrot, shredded

2 cups jicama, shredded

1 small sweet red onion, sliced thinly

¼ cup fresh cilantro, minced

Dressing

½ cup raw, unfiltered apple cider vinegar

½ cup extra virgin olive oil

½ cup fresh pineapple pieces

¼ cup raw honey

1 teaspoon fresh lime juice

¼ cup fresh cilantro leaves

½ teaspoon cumin

½ teaspoon Celtic or Himalayan sea salt

Pinch cayenne (or to taste)

Slaw

Combine all ingredients in large bowl and set aside.

Dressing

Place all ingredients in a Vitamix® and blend until creamy. Pour over slaw and mix well. Refrigerate until served.

Sweet Kale

Sheryll Chavarria, Raw Can Roll Café and Pure Body Spa,
Douglassville, PA (www.rawcanrollcafe.com)

Prep: 20 minutes
Soak: raisins, 1 hour
Yield: 4

3 bunches kale, removed from stem and chopped to desired size
½ cup orange juice
¼ cup sesame oil
2 apples, cored, cut into small pieces
1 cup raisins, soaked and drained
Pinch Celtic sea salt
1–2 tablespoons agave

Combine kale, orange juice, and sesame oil in a large bowl. Massage ingredients together. To massage, you will need to pick up bunches of kale with both hands, squeeze, and rub together relatively vigorously as if you were washing clothes by hand. Kale is ready when it becomes softer in texture. Add remaining ingredients together and serve.

If you have any kale salad left over, you can lay it out on dehydrator sheets and dehydrate at 105°F until crispy (4–6 hours), which turns it into kale chips and makes a great snack.

Un-Marinated Mushrooms

Sheryll Chavarria, Raw Can Roll Café and Pure Body Spa,
Douglassville, PA (www.rawcanrollcafe.com)

Prep: 20 minutes

5–6 zucchini, sliced into medallions
1 tablespoon olive oil
2 tablespoons tamari
½ cup water
2 tablespoons apple cider vinegar
1 clove garlic, pressed
1 tablespoon ginger, grated
1 teaspoon oregano, dried

Mix all ingredients together in a bowl and let sit for at least 15 minutes for the zucchini to absorb the marinade flavor.

This is a great side or can be added to a "Main Event" dish to kick it up.

7-Day Sprout Salad

Brother Viktoras Kulvinskas (Viktoras4u@gmail.com), author of Survival in the 21st Century, *grandfather of raw foods, and co-founder of the Hippocrates Health Institute*

When Viktoras was a speaker at one of my raw potlucks, I was so honored that he would come and share with my potluckers, as well as myself. It was a red-letter day for all of us. Viktoras is extremely knowledgeable, humble, and gracious.

Prep: 30 minutes
Soak: seeds, 8–12 hours

½ up mung beans
½ cup lentils
½ cup alfalfa
¼ cup quinoa
1 teaspoon radish (2 if you like spicy)
1 teaspoon fenugreek seeds, optional

Place all ingredients in your sprout bag. Place the bag in a bowl of water with ½ teaspoon of sea salt. Cover seeds well with water (they will swell). Soak overnight or 8–12 hours, and then drain and rinse thoroughly in fresh water (water should be very clear when finished). Rinse the last time in a basin of ½ gallon of fresh water with ¼ teaspoon of sea salt. Hang bag up to drain, out of the sun. Twice a day, morning and evening, rinse the bag in salted water. Hang to drain afterward. Make sure to shake the bag after rinsing to remove the water. In this fashion, your sprouts will be growing for 7–8 days. The bag will fill with about 10 pounds of sprouts.

. . . continued on next page

They will keep for up to 2 weeks in a plastic bag or glass container in the refrigerator.

This recipe will require a sprout bag or you can use a paint-straining bag that can be purchased at your local hardware store.

You can just eat this sprout salad by itself, add to a "Main Event" dish, or incorporate into your other dishes.

Waldorf Salad

Eric Rivkin, founding member of Jewel of the Sun (a sustainable community in Costa Rica) and founder of the non-profit Viva La Raw Project (www.VivaLaRaw.org), dedicated to health and nutrition education for the masses

Prep: 30 minutes
Soak: walnuts or pecans, 6 hours

2 cups broccoli and cauliflower, cubed into small pieces
3 stalks celery, sliced diagonally
1 cup grapes
1 apple, cubed
1 cup walnuts or pecans, soaked and rinsed
Almond or pine nut mayonnaise (recipe on page 72)

Mix all ingredients together and serve. For variety, use chopped red and white cabbage or fennel bulb.

Almond or Cashew Mayonnaise

Eric Rivkin, founding member of Jewel of the Sun (a sustainable community in Costa Rica) and founder of the non-profit Viva La Raw Project (www.VivaLaRaw.org), dedicated to health and nutrition education for the masses

Prep: 15 minutes
Soak: almonds, 8 hours (or cashews, 4 hours)

1 cup almonds, soaked and rinsed, peeled (if desired), or
    1 cup raw cashews, soaked and rinsed
1 cup water
1 tablespoon raw honey or 2 pitted dates (or other natural
    sweetener)
1 lime or lemon, juiced
Pinch turmeric (for color)
Pinch cayenne
1 tablespoon olive oil

Blend all ingredients (except oil) together in a Vitamix® and drizzle in oil as it is blending until creamy.

Option: substitute pine nuts for half the amount of almonds or cashews.

Tomato Terrine Micro-Greens Salad

Eric Rivkin, founding member of Jewel of the Sun (a sustainable community in Costa Rica) and founder of the non-profit Viva La Raw Project (www.VivaLaRaw.org), dedicated to health and nutrition education for the masses

Prep: 20 minutes

Salad
Large vine-ripened tomatoes
Assortment of micro-greens such as pea shoots, sunflower
        sprouts, mixed field greens, and baby romaine leaves

Dressing
¼ cup olive oil
4 tablespoons lime juice
2 tablespoons honey
1 teaspoon dried red chili flakes
1 clove garlic, crushed
¼–⅓ cup water

Salad
Wash tomatoes and remove stems. Trim the cap off of the top. Carefully scoop out the watery centers with a large spoon, leaving a thick tomato skin to form a cup. Save centers for making a soup or sauce later. Lightly toss the greens with the dressing and fill tomato cups.

Dressing
Combine all ingredients in a Vitamix®.

Pink Sprouted Hummus

Sarah-Jayne Bullock, intuitive health and well-being practitioner focusing on helping people achieve total balance in body, mind, spirit, and life, Towcester, Northamptonshire, UK (www.authentichealthin.com)

Prep: 25 minutes
Soak: sun-dried tomatoes, 30 minutes
Sprout: chickpeas, 1–3 days

2 cups sprouted chickpeas
3–6 sun-dried tomatoes, chopped finely after soaked and
      drained
1½ tablespoon tahini
¼ cup chopped fresh herbs such as basil, chives, and rosemary
1 tablespoon olive or avocado oil
½ medium-sized lemon, juiced
Water, if necessary

Combine ingredients in a food processor until hummus is smooth and creamy. Add additional water and lemon juice until you reach the desired consistency.

Remember: if you add more lemon, the hummus will become more tangy and tart.

Raw Mashed Potatoes with Cauliflower

Alorah Arliotis (www.thewiserwoman.co.uk), Glastonbury, England

Alorah holds sacred retreats in Corfu and Glastonbury to help people find spiritual guidance. Check out her website for more information.

Prep: 25 minutes
Serves: 4

1 heaping cup cashews
1 pound (approximately ⅔ head) raw cauliflower, roughly
    chopped
1 lemon, juiced
1 teaspoon curly leaf parsley, chopped
1 teaspoon soy sauce
¼ cup nutritional yeast
1 tablespoon olive oil
Water, as necessary
Sea salt, to taste
Pepper, to taste

Place cashews, sea salt, and pepper in a food processor, and blend well. Add cauliflower, lemon juice, parsley, soy sauce, and yeast to the food processor, and blend well, adding some purified water in a thin stream if needed to create a smooth consistency. Stop frequently to scrape the container, and add 1 tablespoon of olive oil by drizzling in slowly. Mix until light and fluffy. Chill and serve.

Italian Arugula Salad

Brenda Cobb, founder of Living Foods Institute in Atlanta, GA (www.livingfoodsinstitute.com) and author of The Living Foods Lifestyle

Prep: 20 minutes

Salad
2 cucumbers, chopped and cubed
1 cup red bell pepper, seeded and chopped into cubes
4 cups fresh arugula
1 cup fresh cilantro leaves, chopped

Dressing
2 tablespoons fresh oregano, chopped
1 large clove garlic, minced
3 tablespoons basil, chopped
½ cup extra virgin olive oil
Pinch cayenne pepper
½ cup fresh lemon juice
1 teaspoon Himalayan sea salt

Salad
Combine all ingredients in a large bowl.

Dressing
Place all ingredients in a Vitamix® and blend until creamy. Add the dressing to the salad right before you are ready to serve.

Thai Green Mango Salad

Sheryll Chavarria, Raw Can Roll Café and Pure Body Spa,
Douglassville, PA (www.rawcanrollcafe.com)

Prep: 25 minutes

Salad
2 firm mangos (must not be ripe), shredded
¼ cup dry, shredded unsweetened coconut
2 cups bean sprouts
1 tablespoon coriander
3 scallions, chopped
⅓ cup fresh basil, chopped
Handful peanuts, set aside

Dressing
3 tablespoons tamari
3–4 tablespoons lime or lemon juice, freshly squeezed
2 tablespoons orange juice
2 tablespoons agave, to taste (can add more)
1–2 tablespoons sesame oil
Pinch cayenne pepper (optional)

Salad
In a large mixing bowl, toss all ingredients (except for the peanuts).

Dressing
In a separate small mixing bowl, whisk together all ingredients. Pour salad dressing over the salad and toss lightly. Garnish with peanuts.

MAIN EVENT

The "Main Event" is the drum-roll moment of any party or gathering and a raw potluck is no different. Yes, the dessert will be the icing on the cake (every pun intended), but the "Main Event" dishes will have your guests talking about your party for weeks.

Asian Butternut Noodles

Alorah Arliotis (www.thewiserwoman.co.uk), Glastonbury, England

Alorah holds sacred retreats in Corfu and Glastonbury to help people find spiritual guidance. Check out her website for more information.

Prep: 30 minutes

½ medium butternut squash, peeled and seeded
1 tablespoon olive oil
½ teaspoon sea salt
3 tablespoons shredded coconut
½ teaspoon curry powder
¼ teaspoon chili powder
½ teaspoon turmeric
¼ teaspoon ginger powder
Splash of water
2 teaspoons agave nectar
Sprouted green lentils or alfalfa sprouts for garnish

After you have peeled and seeded the butternut squash, use your spiralizer to make the noodles. Place the noodles in a mixing bowl, and drizzle with olive oil and sea salt. Toss to coat and set aside.

In a small bowl, combine coconut, curry, chili, turmeric, and ginger, and then mix.

Add a splash of water and mix well. Now, mash mixture with a spoon. Add mix and agave to noodles. Toss well with a fork or your hands to mix evenly. Serve alone or with a green salad of romaine lettuce and cilantro tossed with a sweet-and-sour dressing (olive oil, apple cider vinegar, orange juice, and agave). Garnish with green lentils or alfalfa sprouts.

Spring Goddess Salad

Potlucker Janice Innella, The Beauty Chef, Philadelphia, PA

Janice is known for her Goddess events, and this salad was featured as a "Main Event" at her Spring, 2011, "Goddess in the Kitchen" class. I have been blessed to take Janice's classes through the years.

Prep: 40 minutes

1 head bok choy, chopped

1 head Swiss chard, chopped

1 bunch asparagus, chopped (save 4 spears for garnish)

1 fresh fennel bulb, chopped

1 bunch fresh dill, chopped

1 medium onion, peeled and chopped

1 green apple, seeded and chopped (optional)

2 ribs celery, chopped

4 tablespoons hemp seeds

8 ounces strawberries, sliced

Clean and hand-chop all your ingredients (except strawberries), and mix together. Arrange in a beautiful wooden bowl with strawberries decorated around the top. Serves 6.

You can use a food processor to chop the onion, apple, and dill.

Coconut-Dill-Kefir Dressing
(for Goddess Salad)

Potlucker Janice Innella, The Beauty Chef, Philadelphia, PA

Prep: 10 minutes

1 cup Coconut Kefir (see recipe on page 83)
3 tablespoons fresh dill
2 ounces raw cashews
3 tablespoons olive oil
2 tablespoons fresh lemon juice
2 tablespoons red onion

Blend all ingredients together in a Vitamix®.

You can pour this dressing on the Spring Goddess Salad (see page 81), making sure that you mix thoroughly through the salad, or you can serve the dressing on the side.

Coconut Kefir

Potlucker Janice Innella, The Beauty Chef, Philadelphia, PA

This is one of Janice's favorite beautifying foods, because it helps to make your skin, hair, and nails radiate. Just drink 4 ounces a day or more. For more medicinal effects, drink 1 quart each day and watch your belly fat dissolve and your thyroid, if underactive, regulate (along with many other benefits). Janice does drink this regularly and has personally noticed her thyroid regulate and belly fat dissolve. See Donna Gates' book The Body Ecology Diet *for more information (*The Body Ecology Diet *is one of the first books I read when I changed my diet originally because of food allergies).*

Prep: 15 minutes

1 pack Body Ecology™ Kefir Starter
4 young coconuts, meat and water
1 tablespoon raw honey

Combine all ingredients in your Vitamix® and blend until blender becomes warm. Pour into a 2-gallon jar, wrap in towel, and then place in a very warm part of your kitchen (for example, in the middle of the stove where the pilot light is). You are fermenting now so you want the temperature to be around 80°F. This works perfectly in the summertime. Ferment for 36 hours. The kefir will rise and separate, the fat will rise to the top, and the liquid will sink to the bottom.

Very carefully open your kefir (you will hear a hissing sound). This is a live-fermented product so, if you shake the jar, it will explode. I do not mean to scare you, but this did happen to me in the summer. A jar broke in my hand, I poured the kefir right on it,

. . . continued on next page

and it healed within 3 days. Much care and mindfulness needs to happen when preparing this fermented product.

You can find Body Ecology™ Kefir Starter online or in the refrigerated sections of your health store.

Sprouted Veggie Burgers

Potlucker Janice Innella, The Beauty Chef, Philadelphia, PA

Prep: 40 minutes
Sprout: beans, 3–5 days
Dehydrate: 4 hours each side at 115°F

2 cups sprouted beans (mung, adjuki, lentil, pea)
1 cup hemp seeds
⅔ cup golden flax seeds, ground
1 cup red onion
1 shallot
3 scallions
⅓ cup sun-dried tomato paste*
2 tablespoons olive oil
1 small green zucchini
2 tablespoons fresh parsley
2 tablespoons fresh basil
2 tablespoons chives
1 teaspoon kelp powder
2 teaspoons Himalayan sea salt
½ cup pure water
2 ribs celery, hand-chopped small
½ red pepper, hand-chopped small

Combine all ingredients, except red pepper and celery, into your food processor and pulse until blended together. Add everything (including red pepper and celery) to a bowl with ½ cup of pure water. Hand-mix.

. . . continued on next page

Form patties by hand about 2-x-2-inches. Recipe will yield about 6–8. Dehydrate at 115°F each side for 4 hours. Make sure that the patties are soft on the inside and firm on the outside.

Serve patties on top of your favorite salad or sandwich with your favorite raw condiments and lettuce, avocado, red onion, and tomato. Will last in your refrigerator for 3 days. Freeze extra for another meal.

*Soak 1 cup of sun-dried tomatoes in enough water to cover for 20 minutes. After soaking, combine the tomatoes, soaking water, and one jalapeño pepper (cleaned and seeded) in a Vitamix® blender until well-blended.

Barbecue Sauce

Potlucker Janice Innella, The Beauty Chef, Philadelphia, PA

Prep: 15 minutes
Soak: sun-dried tomatoes, 1 hour

1 cup sun-dried tomatoes, soaked, save soaking water
1 teaspoon chipolata spice, or more for extra heat
1 teaspoon jalapeño, seeds removed
1 teaspoon fresh ground cumin
1 clove garlic
2 tablespoons fresh lemon juice
2 tablespoons olive oil
1 shallot
Pinch Himalayan sea salt

Combine all ingredients in a Vitamix® and blend until smooth. The barbecue sauce will last in a refrigerator in a sealed, air-tight container for 10 days–2 weeks.

This makes a great condiment for Sprouted Veggie Burgers (see page 85).

Raw Mustard

Potlucker Janice Innella, The Beauty Chef, Philadelphia, PA

Prep: 10 minutes

3 tablespoons fresh ground mustard seeds
2 tablespoons olive oil
Few drops of fresh lemon juice
Pinch Himalayan sea salt

Combine ingredients in a mixing bowl or in a mortar and pestle, and blend together well.

This makes a great condiment for Sprouted Veggie Burgers (see page 85).

Pine-Nut Cheese Chunks

Potlucker Janice Innella, The Beauty Chef, Philadelphia, PA

Prep: 15 minutes
Dehydrate: 4 hours each side at 115°F

1 cup raw pine nuts
2 tablespoons lemon juice
½ teaspoon Himalayan sea salt
3 tablespoons nutritional yeast (optional)
6 tablespoons water

Blend ingredients together in a Vitamix®, spread on Teflex sheets, and dehydrate at 115°F for 4 hours on each side. Store in refrigerator for 2 weeks (I have also stored these in sealed glass jars; they also make a great snack).

This makes a great condiment for Sprouted Veggie Burgers (see page 85).

Walnut Flatbread for Veggie Burger

Potlucker Janice Innella, The Beauty Chef, Philadelphia, PA

Prep: 25 minutes
Soak: walnuts, overnight or 6 hours
Dehydrate: 14 hours at 115°F

1½ cups golden flax seeds, ground fresh

2 cups pure water

3 cups raw walnuts, soaked, drained, and rinsed

1 teaspoon sea salt

3 tablespoons fresh chives

3 tablespoons raw sesame seeds

1 tablespoon olive oil

Combine ground flax seeds and water in a large bowl, and set aside. In a food processor, add all of the remaining ingredients and pulse/grind until batter becomes smooth. Combine all ingredients in a large bowl with flax seeds. Hand-mix the batter for a few minutes.

With your hands, take about 4 ounces of batter and mold into balls, then flatten out on a dehydrator sheet so the dough forms round flatbread circles. Dehydrate at 115°F for 6 hours, flip, remove the Teflex sheets, and dry for another 8 hours or until bread is completely dry (plan meal ahead when putting this recipe together). The bread should be a bit flexible for your burger. Store in an air-tight, dry container. If you leave the bread moist, then store in the refrigerator. Air-tight bread will last for 6 weeks in the freezer. If storing in the refrigerator, the bread will last for 2 weeks. This batter should make 12 or more flatbread rounds. You can adjust size and flavorings to your liking.

You are now ready to build your burger (see page 85) into a

beautiful presentation. Start with flatbread, and top with raw condiments (pine-nut cheese, sauce, red onion, avocado, lettuce, sprouts), then close with another flatbread. Serve with your favorite side salad.

Veggie Collard Wraps

Sheryll Chavarria, Raw Can Roll Café and Pure Body Spa,
Douglassville, PA (www.rawcanrollcafe.com)

Prep: 30 minutes

Marinade
1 tablespoon ginger, ground fresh
2 cloves garlic, pressed
2 tablespoons tamari
2 tablespoons lemon juice
2 tablespoons sesame oil

Wrap
1 Portobello mushroom, sliced and marinated
4 collard greens, de-stemmed
4 snow peas
2 carrots, ribboned
2 cups Napa cabbage, cut fine
1 cucumber, julienned

Marinade
Combine all ingredients.

Wrap
Marinate the mushrooms for about 15 minutes. Squeeze out excess marinade back into bowl and set aside to use later as a sauce.

Place the remaining ingredients in the collard leaf and roll. Wrap and secure the roll with a strip of carrot and a toothpick.

Use the remaining marinade for dipping or pour on wrap before you wrap the collard.

Picadillo

*Co-Potluck Hostess Linda Leboutillier, Waterloo Gardens, Exton/
Devon, PA*

*When Linda made this for lunch for me one day, I was blown away. The
serving says that it yields 4–6, but this is so good that you could eat it
all yourself. I just loved it.*

Prep: 40 minutes
Soak: pecans, 6 hours; walnuts, 6 hours

Nut and Spice
2½ cups pecans, soaked, drained, and dehydrated
2½ cups walnuts, soaked, drained, and dehydrated
4 tablespoons Frontier™ Pizza Seasoning
¾ tablespoon paprika
2 teaspoons dried oregano
½ teaspoon clove garlic, minced
Pinch of cayenne
1 tablespoon of kelp powder or 3 tablespoons Bragg® Liquid
    Aminos
2 teaspoons mesquite
½ teaspoon cumin
½ teaspoon black pepper

Vegetables
2½ cups red pepper, diced
2½ cups yellow squash, diced
1 cup red onion, diced
¼ cup lime juice
½ cup fresh parsley, chopped

. . . continued on next page

1 cup green olives, chopped
1 cup corn, cut from cob
1½ cups tomatoes, chopped
2 bay leaves (remove upon serving)
¼ cup raisins
2 teaspoons capers
1 (2¼ ounce) can black olives, drained and chopped

Nut and Spice
Pulse all ingredients in a food processor.

Vegetables
Combine all ingredients in a large mixing bowl with the first mixture.

Serve on a bed of greens.

Purple and Yellow Egg

Potlucker Linda Cooper, Linda Louise Cakes, Harleysville, PA

Linda created this dish, made it for an Easter raw potluck, and it was a hit. You can make this dish any time of the year, because it does not have to be made in the shape of eggs.

Prep: 45 minutes

Purple Egg
1 cup yellow squash
½ cup zucchini
1½ cups celery
1 cup green cabbage
1 cup purple cabbage
½ teaspoon dill
¼ teaspoon dehydrated green onion powder
Couple sprigs parsley
2–3 tablespoons raw almond butter
Sea salt, to taste

Yellow Egg
1 cup yellow squash
½ cup zucchini
1½ cups celery
1 cup green cabbage
½ cup Napa cabbage
1 cup carrots
Sprig fresh basil
1 avocado

. . . continued on next page

1 kiwi, chopped

¼ cup pineapple, chopped, plus ¼ cup, chopped

Purple Egg

Combine all of the ingredients (except almond butter) in a food processor with an "S" blade and pulse to a fine chop. Transfer to a bowl and stir in 2–3 tablespoons raw almond butter. Form mixture into a large egg and serve on a platter of greens or shredded cabbage.

Yellow Egg

Finely chop the squash, zucchini, celery, cabbage, carrots, and basil in a food processor using an "S" blade. Transfer mixture to a bowl. Blend together the avocado, kiwi, and pineapple by hand, and stir by hand into the yellow egg mixture. Finely chop another ¼ cup pineapple and add to mixture by hand. Form into a large yellow egg, and serve on a platter of greens and cabbages.

Walnut Steak

Brenda Cobb, founder of Living Foods Institute in Atlanta, GA (www.livingfoodsinstitute.com) and author of The Living Foods Lifestyle

Prep: 25 minutes
Soak: walnuts, sunflower seeds, and almonds, overnight
Dehydrate: 2 hours at 100°F

1 cup walnuts, soaked
½ cup sunflower seeds, soaked
½ cup almonds, soaked
3 medjool dates, pitted and soaked
5 cups water
3 cloves garlic
¼ tablespoon Himalayan salt
¼ cup onion
1 tablespoon fresh rosemary
½ cup red bell pepper
1 teaspoon fresh jalapeño pepper, seeded
¾ teaspoon cumin
1 cup fresh tomatoes
2 tablespoons fresh basil leaves

Soak the walnuts, sunflower seeds, almonds, and dates in 5 cups of water overnight, and then drain. Combine the remaining ingredients in the food processor using an "S" blade. Then add the walnuts, sunflower seeds, and almonds to the mixture in the food processor, and blend into a chunky mixture.

Form into patties, dehydrate at 100°F for 2 hours, and serve warm.

Sprouted Sunflower Seed Pâté
(Tuna-less Salad)

Potlucker Chef Barbara Shevkun, Rawfully Tempting
(www.rawfullytempting.com)

When Barbara brought this dish to our raw potluck, it was the hit of the night. It was the first dish to be eaten so you know that it was a huge success.

Prep: 25 minutes
Soak: sunflower seeds, 4–6 hours
Almonds, overnight

1½ cups sunflower seeds, soaked
½ cup almonds, soaked overnight
¼ cup water (or more as needed)
1 clove garlic, crushed
½ cup celery, chopped
¼–½ cup red onion, finely chopped
2 tablespoons fresh parsley, chopped
1 teaspoon dried dill
2 tablespoons olive oil
1 tablespoon coconut water vinegar (or your favorite vinegar)
1 tablespoon dulse flakes (optional)
¼ teaspoon sea salt (or to taste)

Rinse and drain soaked nuts and seeds, and then process in a food processor, adding water as needed. Mix until mixture is similar to tuna-salad consistency. Transfer to a bowl and add remaining ingredients. Serve on raw flax crackers, bread, or lettuce wraps. Garnish with sliced tomato, avocado, and red onion.

Sushi Roll

Potluckers Bruce and Marsha Weinstein, Awesome Foods, Bridgeport, PA (www.awesomefoods.com)

Bruce and Marsha's veggie nori rolls were the hit of the potluck.

Prep: 40 minutes
Dehydrate: 3 hours at 115°F
Yield: Makes 3 (3 ounce) rolls

Veggies
1 ounce carrots, shredded
1 ounce yellow pepper, thinly sliced
1 ounce red pepper, thinly sliced
1 ounce celery, thinly sliced
½ ounce scallions, thinly sliced
0.3 ounce olive oil
0.2 ounce lemon juice
⅛ teaspoon sea salt

Sushi Rice
26 ounces jicama
0.4 ounce apple cider vinegar
1.1 ounces extra virgin olive oil
0.7 ounce agave nectar
½ ounce Himalayan sea salt

Veggies
Combine veggies in a bowl so they are thoroughly coated with the olive oil, lemon juice, and sea salt, and set aside.

. . . continued on next page

Sushi Rice

Shred the jicama in a food processor until it is the consistency of rice grains. Press the chopped jicama in batches into thick towels inside a colander to remove the juice. Combine the jicama with the other ingredients in a bowl. Spread out on parchment paper or Teflex sheets, and place in your dehydrator for 3 hours at 115°F. After you dehydrate, you should have about 5 ounces (by weight).

Assembly

Spread 1.4 ounces (by weight) of rice on bottom half of nori sheets. Nori weighs 0.1 ounces, so now you have 1.5 ounces. Lay 1.5 ounces of marinated veggies on rice. Roll up and put face down on paper towel or sushi bamboo mat. Total weight is 3 ounces. Cut each roll into 6 pieces.

Chili Con Amore (With Love)

Sheryll Chavarria, Raw Can Roll Café and Pure Body Spa,
Douglassville, PA (www.rawcanrollcafe.com)

Prep: 25 minutes
Soak: sun-dried tomatoes, 1 hour

1 cup zucchini, chopped

1 large Portobello mushroom, chopped

1 cup corn, cut off cob

½ cup green beans, chopped (optional)

1 cup fresh tomatoes, chopped

1 red bell pepper, chopped finely

½ cup red onion, chopped finely

1–2 tablespoons jalapeño, chopped very finely (optional)

1 tablespoon cumin powder

1 tablespoon chili powder

2 tablespoons tamari

2 cloves garlic

3 tablespoons olive oil

1 cup sun-dried tomatoes, soaked (keep approximately 1 cup
   soaking water)

Combine the zucchini, mushroom, corn, green beans, tomatoes, pepper, onion, and jalapeño (optional) in a mixing bowl and set aside. Blend remaining ingredients together. Mix with chopped veggies in a bowl. Take about ¼ of the mixture out and blend to create a juicier chili. Place back into bowl. This chili can also be warmed in a dehydrator. Top with a spoonful of Chipotle Sour Cream (see page 102) and serve.

Chipotle Sour Cream

Sheryll Chavarria, Raw Can Roll Café and Pure Body Spa, Douglassville, PA (www.rawcanrollcafe.com)

I made this recipe on air on WFMZ TV, Channel 69, in Allentown, PA, on April 1, 2011, and the crew loved it.

Prep: 25 minutes

3 tomatoes, chopped (preferably plum/Roma tomatoes)
1 mango, peeled and pitted
¼ cup onion, chopped fine
½ bunch cilantro, chopped fine
½ lemon or lime, juiced
½ jalapeño pepper, chopped fine (optional)
1–2 cloves garlic, minced
Sea salt, to taste

Combine all ingredients together in a Vitamix® high-speed blender.

Serve as a sauce on the Chili Con Amore (see page 101). This can also be used as a dip. You can even dehydrate the mixture, turn it into crackers or pour it over broccoli cut into bite-sized pieces, place in a glass Pyrex® dish, and dehydrate until warm.

Maki-Sushi Rolls with "Rawsmati" Ryce

Eric Rivkin, founding member of Jewel of the Sun (a sustainable community in Costa Rica) and founder of the non-profit Viva La Raw Project (www.VivaLaRaw.org), dedicated to health and nutrition education for the masses

A living substitute for sticky vinegared rice and tastes so much better.

Prep: 35 minutes

Basic Rawsmati Ryce
½ cup pine nuts, cashews, or macadamias nuts
½ cup fresh coconut meat, chopped
2 cups fresh palm hearts (palmito), chopped
1 large jicama, peeled and chopped
1 lime, juiced
¼ cup cilantro leaves
1 teaspoon curry
½ teaspoon coriander

Sushi Roll Filling
1 sheet untoasted nori
1 green onion or chives, chopped
1 avocado, sliced
1 apple, sliced thinly
1 cucumber, julienned
1 red bell pepper, julienned
1 carrot, julienned
Alfalfa sprouts
Spinach or soft lettuce leaves

. . . continued on next page

Basic Rawsmati Ryce

Using the "S" blade of your food processor, finely chop the nuts. Scrape down, and then add the coconut meat, palm hearts, and jicama root. Pulse-chop until you get a sticky, coarse texture. Then briefly pulse in the lime juice, cilantro leaves, curry, and coriander.

Sushi Roll Filling

Lay flat a bamboo sushi mat and place a sheet of nori shiny-side-down on the bamboo mat. Spread a heaping serving spoon of Rawsmati Ryce onto the nori, covering ½ of the surface about ⅛-inch thick. Layer a few of the various ingredients, finishing with the spinach or lettuce leaves. Roll up firmly, but gently, and seal the last ½-inch with water. Slice into 1-inch long pieces and serve with Tamarind Sauce (see page 105) or one of the many sauces in Eric's book, *To LIVE For*.

Tamarind Sauce

Eric Rivkin, founding member of Jewel of the Sun (a sustainable community in Costa Rica) and founder of the non-profit Viva La Raw Project (www.VivaLaRaw.org), dedicated to health and nutrition education for the masses

Prep: 20 minutes
Soak: tamarind pulp and seeds, 1 day

¾ cup tamarind paste, made to instructions below
¼ cup pitted dates or local honey, as needed to balance
      sweetness
1 cup coconut water or purified water
1–2 oranges, juiced
1 lime, juiced
1 red bell pepper
½ teaspoon cumin
1-inch knuckle of fresh ginger root
½ cup ripe mango (optional)
½ cup soft coconut meat (optional)
Hot chili pepper, to taste

Tamarind is available either fresh in the pod or as a paste with the pits. If in the pod, remove the shell and tough fibers surrounding the sticky flesh. For both types, soak the pulp and seeds for 1 day in just enough purified water to cover. Saving the soaking water, remove the softened pulp from the seeds with your fingertips and set aside. Discard the seeds. Blend together the tamarind pulp, soak water, and all other ingredients until smooth. Stores refrigerated in glass jars up to 4 days.

Open Lasagna

Eric Rivkin, founding member of Jewel of the Sun (a sustainable community in Costa Rica) and founder of the non-profit Viva La Raw Project (www.VivaLaRaw.org), dedicated to health and nutrition education for the masses

Prep: 60 minutes
Soak: macadamias or cashews, 8 hours

Marinara Sauce
5 ripe Roma or other medium-sized tomatoes
6–10 sun-dried tomatoes
5–8 strawberries
¼ cup golden raisins, 2 dried figs, or 2 medjool dates (pitted)
2 sprigs thyme leaves
1 tablespoon fresh oregano
¼ cup fresh basil, packed
1 clove garlic
2 green onions
1 teaspoon minced jalapeño or cayenne, to taste
¼ teaspoon cinnamon

Ricotta Spread
1 cup raw macadamias or cashews, soaked, drained, and rinsed
2 cloves garlic
1 lemon or lime, juiced
1 teaspoon raw honey
2 tablespoons raw tahini
Fresh oregano, basil, dill, or thyme (optional), to taste
Water, as necessary

Lasagna

1 large Portobello mushroom, sliced in strips across as thin
      as possible

2 cloves garlic, minced

1 tablespoon olive oil

½ lemon, juiced

1 tablespoon fresh oregano, minced

¼ cup fresh basil, chopped

1 tablespoon fresh thyme, minced

1 tablespoon fresh dill, minced

5 zucchinis, sliced lengthwise on a mandolin 1.5 millimeters
      or less

1 red bell pepper, diced

1 cup spinach (or greens of your choice), chopped

Marinara Sauce

Blend ingredients together until smooth in a Vitamix® high-speed blender and set aside.

Ricotta Spread

Puree ingredients in blender until fluffy and thick, adding water as necessary. Set aside.

Assembly

Marinate mushrooms in the garlic, olive oil, lemon juice, oregano, basil, thyme, and dill.

    Start with the zucchini slices, and lay them out on a plate or in a glass lasagna pan. Alternate ricotta spread, marinated mushrooms, marinara sauce, red bell pepper, chopped spinach, and greens. Serve immediately.

Ratatouille

Lisa Montgomery

Prep: 40 minutes

16 ounces Roma tomatoes
1 yellow squash, chopped
1 zucchini, chopped
1 red bell pepper, chopped
1 yellow pepper, chopped
1 orange pepper, chopped
1 eggplant, cubed
1–2 large Portobello mushrooms, chopped
1 red onion, chopped or ringed
2 cloves garlic, minced
2 teaspoons dried parsley
2 teaspoons dried oregano
2 tablespoons olive oil
½ cup orange juice
Sea salt, to taste
Ground pepper, to taste

Pulse-chop tomatoes in food processor so they look like stewed tomatoes, and set aside. Chop remaining vegetables and combine with tomatoes in a large mixing bowl. Add seasonings to mixture and thoroughly coat. Add more olive oil to make sure that all vegetables are covered. Place ratatouille in large glass dish and place in dehydrator until warm. Stir occasionally to make sure the flavors are all melding together. Serve on a bed of greens.

DESSERTS

The easiest way to get people to go raw is to serve them raw deserts (of course, you never tell them that the deserts are raw). Whenever I do a book signing, I also make a dessert and give tastings. People think that if you are going to eat healthy, you can never have another dessert, again. Or if it's a healthy dessert, they assume that it will taste like cardboard. Many people also think that they will never have chocolate again on a healthy diet. With just one mouthful of any of these desserts, people's eyes begin to light up, and you can see the smile come across their face. They have no idea desserts can be healthy, taste great, be good for you, and actually be easy to make.

Dr. D's Simple Dessert
Dr. Doug Graham, author of 80/10/10

Prep: 15 minutes

Mango, peeled and cored
2–4 leaves chocolate mint
Pinch vanilla

In a Vitamix®, blend together mango with chocolate mint and vanilla. Chill and serve.

Feel-Good Fudge

Potlucker Sally Bowdle, Sally B Gluten Free (www.sallybglutenfree.com)

Prep: 20 minutes

¼ cup almond butter
¼ cup agave syrup
2 tablespoons coconut oil
¼ cup cacao powder
Pinch salt

In a double boiler, gently warm the almond butter, agave syrup, and coconut oil, and melt together until smooth. Remember to warm the chocolate at less than 118°F. Sift in the cacao powder and salt. Mix until smooth.

This can be used as a sauce over a dessert or can be poured into tiny candy-cup liners set in a mini-muffin tray. Freeze for 1 hour, and you have the perfect one-bite dessert treat. You can also pour into an 8-x-8-inch pan lined with parchment, freeze, and cut into squares.

Chocolate Cheesecake

Sheryll Chavarria, Raw Can Roll Café and Pure Body Spa,
Douglassville, PA (www.rawcanrollcafe.com)

Prep: 30 minutes
Soak: cashews, 1 hour

Crust
2 cups raw walnuts
½ cup dates, pitted
¼ cup dried coconut

Cheese
2 cups cashew, soaked
½ cup agave
½ cup coconut oil, warmed
1 tablespoon vanilla
Pinch–¼ teaspoon Celtic sea salt
¼ cup warm water
½–¾ cup cacao nibs
1 tablespoon cacao powder

Crust
Process the walnuts and dates in a food processor. Sprinkle dried coconut onto bottom of pie plate (the dried coconut keeps the crust from sticking to the pie plate, which makes it easier to get the pie out of the plate). Press crust onto the coconut.

Cheese
Blend cashews, agave, gently warmed coconut oil (see note), vanilla, sea salt, and water in a high-speed blender. Blend until smooth. Mix in the cacao nibs. Pour the mixture onto the crust.

Remove air bubbles by tapping the pan on the table. Sprinkle cacao powder over top of pie. Place in the freezer until firm. Defrost in the refrigerator.

Warm coconut oil by placing in a glass Pyrex® dish, and place in a bowl of hot water.

Coconut Silk/Chocolate-Lined Pie with Strawberries

Sheryll Chavarria, Raw Can Roll Café and Pure Body Spa, Douglassville, PA (www.rawcanrollcafe.com)

Prep: 20 minutes

2 cups young Thai coconut meat
1 tablespoon vanilla
¼–½ cup agave
¼ cup coconut oil
Pinch Celtic sea salt
Coconut milk/water (as much as needed, but not much)
2 cups strawberries (ornamentally sliced and fanned with
      tops on)

In your Vitamix® high-speed blender, blend coconut meat starting with 1 cup, add all other ingredients (except strawberries) until creamy, and then add the rest of the coconut meat and continue blending until creamy. Fill pie crust, top with fanned strawberries, and refrigerate or put in freezer for about 20 minutes to set.

Raw Chocolate Crust

Sheryll Chavarria, Raw Can Roll Café and Pure Body Spa,
Douglassville, PA (www.rawcanrollcafe.com)

Prep: 15 minutes

¾ cup cacao
½ cup agave
Pinch Celtic sea salt
½ teaspoon vanilla, mint, or any other flavoring you would like
¼ cup coconut oil, melted

Place all ingredients into a bowl and stir, adding the coconut oil last. Chocolate will set up quickly, especially in cooler weather. Pour raw chocolate into a pie dish and let set in freezer for 20 minutes. Take crust from freezer, pour in coconut-cream filling (see Coconut Silk/Chocolate-Lined Pie on page 114), top with sliced strawberries, and sprinkle with coconut flakes.

Almond-Coconut Macaroons

Sheryll Chavarria, Raw Can Roll Café and Pure Body Spa,
Douglassville, PA (www.rawcanrollcafe.com)

Prep: 20 minutes
Dehydrate: 6 hours at 115°F

2½ cups coconut (unsweetened and dried)
1¼ cups almond flour (finely ground dried raw almonds)
¾ cup agave
¼ cup coconut butter/oil, melted
1 tablespoon vanilla
1 pinch Celtic sea salt

Mix all ingredients together in a mixing bowl. Form into small balls
and place on dehydrator sheets (you may eat them un-dehydrated,
as well). Dehydrate at 115°F for up to 6 hours.

Raw Chocolate Candies

Sheryll Chavarria, Raw Can Roll Café and Pure Body Spa,
Douglassville, PA (www.rawcanrollcafe.com)

Prep: 20 minutes

½ cup cacao
¼ cup agave
Pinch Celtic sea salt
½ teaspoon vanilla
¼ cup coconut oil, melted and warm
2 drops mint, lavender, orange, or any other flavoring you
        like (optional)

Place all ingredients into a bowl and mix, adding the coconut oil
last. Chocolate will set up quickly, especially in cooler weather.
Immediately pour into candy mold forms and place in freezer for
20 minutes.

You can get creative and place a dab of almond butter or cashew
butter in the center for a creamy filling.

Lemon Squares

Sheryll Chavarria, Raw Can Roll Café and Pure Body Spa,
Douglassville, PA (www.rawcanrollcafe.com)

Prep: 25 minutes

4 cups walnuts or pecans, un-soaked
2 cups raisins or pitted dates, un-soaked
3 bananas
2 lemons

Process walnuts and raisins in food processor. Process until the walnuts and raisins stick together. Take out and press the walnut-raisin mixture into the dish.

Slice bananas and set aside. Juice lemons and grate the peel of 1 lemon. Put banana slices on top of crust and pour the lemon juice on top of bananas. Garnish with the lemon peel. Refrigerate, cut into squares, and serve.

Coffee-Pecan Ice Cream

Potlucker Linda Cooper, Linda Louise Cakes, Harleysville, PA

This is a rich, buttery-tasting frozen treat. Better than butter pecan ice cream any day, with just a hint of coffee. I do not like coffee, but I really liked this when Linda brought it to the potluck.

Prep: 30 minutes
Soak: pecans, 4 hours

2½ cups pecans, soaked and dehydrated
1 young Thai coconut (meat and water)
½ cup raw Coconut Secret® Coconut Nectar
¼ teaspoon sea salt
4 drops Medicine Flower® Coffee Flavor Extract
1 drop Medicine Flower® Vanilla Flavor Extract
3 drops liquid vanilla stevia
1 whole flexible organic vanilla bean, cut into several pieces
½ tablespoon sunflower lecithin
½ cup coconut oil, melted

Combine all ingredients (except sunflower lecithin and melted coconut oil) into a high-speed blender and blend well (several minutes; do not overheat). Stir the sunflower lecithin into the melted coconut oil and incorporate into the first mixture, blending well. Pour into a glass container with a lid and freeze overnight. Enjoy like ice cream.

Raw Almond and Cherry Cookies

Alorah Arliotis (www.thewiserwoman.co.uk), Glastonbury, England

Alorah holds sacred retreats in Corfu and Glastonbury to help people find spiritual guidance. Check out her website for more information.

Prep: 35 minutes
Soak: almonds, 8–12 hours
Dehydrate: almonds, 8 hours or overnight at 105°F

1½ cups raw almonds, soaked, drained, and dehydrated
        until dry
¼ teaspoon freshly ground nutmeg
¼ teaspoon sea salt
2 teaspoons agave syrup
½-¾ cup raw cacao powder
1 cup dried cherries
¼ teaspoon pure almond extract
½ teaspoon vanilla extract
1 tablespoon hemp seed oil
1 tablespoon hulled hemp seeds

Place 1 cup of almonds in food processor, and then pulse almonds, nutmeg, sea salt, agave syrup, and cacao until coarsely chopped. Add cherries and extracts, and pulse until mixture comes together, but is still chunky. Place in a small mixing bowl, and combine with hemp oil and seeds. Set aside.

Grind remaining ½ cup of almonds in a coffee grinder until finely ground. Set aside.

Form mixture into balls and roll into almond meal. Chill for at least 2 hours and serve. Store in sealed, airtight container.

Banana-Strawberry-Nut Cobbler

Brenda Cobb, founder of Living Foods Institute in Atlanta, GA (www.livingfoodsinstitute.com) and author of The Living Foods Lifestyle

Prep: 25 minutes
Soak: walnuts, overnight

1 cup walnuts, soaked and drained
4 ripe bananas
6 pitted medjool dates
3 cups strawberries
1 tablespoon fresh lemon juice
2 cups shredded coconut

Soak the walnuts in 3 cups water overnight and drain. Chop the bananas, dates, 2 cups of the strawberries, and walnuts, and then toss with the lemon juice. Add in the coconut and blend together. Serve in small dessert dishes and decorate the top with the remaining sliced strawberries.

Winter Citrus Zippies

Potlucker Denise DiJoseph (www.miaura.com)

These cashew and pine nut cookies have a zip of citrus flavor.

Prep: 45 minutes
Soak: cashews, 4 hours
Dehydrate: cashews, 5 hours (or until dry) at 105°F; cookies,
8 hours at 105–110°F or until you reach a desired soft/chewy
texture without making them dry and/or crunchy
Yield: 24–30 cookies

Cookie Base

2 cups raw cashews, ground to a fine powder in grinder (soaked
    and dehydrated in advance)

¼ cup agave nectar

2½ tablespoons finely grated peel from organic lemon

3 tablespoons lemon juice

1 organic vanilla bean, cut into pieces and ground up in a
    grinder (reserve half for cookie centers)

¼ teaspoon natural salt (I use Redmond Natural™)

Cookie Center

About ⅛ cup lucuma powder

2 tablespoons maca powder

About ⅛ cup mesquite powder

1 tablespoon Amazing Grass® Green SuperFood Powder™

1 tablespoon cacao powder (optional)

Remainder of ground vanilla bean from cookie base

About ⅛–¼ cup pine-nut butter (or other nut butter: I use raw
    pine nuts and a grinder to make pine-nut butter)

Filtered water, as necessary

1 soft raisin to top each cookie

Cookie Marinade
1 organic orange and rind

Cookie Base
Combine all ingredients in a small food processor to form a dough-like consistency. Using a hinged melon baller, scoop out cookie dough and place on a Teflex sheet. Roll each cookie into a ball and flatten down to form a flattened circle.

Cookie Center
Combine all ingredients (except for raisins) in a small food processor and add just enough water to form a dough-ball consistency. Scoop out enough dough to roll into a large pea-sized ball. Take 1 raisin and add it to the ball while rolling out. Place each ball on top of the flattened round cookies from above, and then pat down so the base and center are gently joined. Refrigerate overnight on a Teflex sheet.

Cookie Marinade
Juice the orange with the Tribest® CitraStar Juicer. Brush the orange juice on each cookie with a pastry brush (brush the cookies so they glisten, but not so much that they become soggy). Slice the rind into very thin slivers and garnish each cookie. Remove each cookie from the Teflex sheet with a spatula, and place each on an open-grid dehydrator shelf. Dehydrate under 110°F until desired consistency.

Katharine's Raw Brownies

Katherine Clark (Healthworkshi@gmail.com, www.kclark.biz)

Prep: 45 minutes
Soak: dates, 1 hour

2 cups Brazil nuts, ground into meal

2¼ cups cacao powder (finely ground if using nibs)

2 tablespoons Sunfood Nutrition™ Maca Extreme Powder

2 tablespoons APA Blend by Simplexity®

2 tablespoons Simply SBGA by Simplexity®

2 cups sweetener (agave, raw honey, yacon, or soaked dates and
        date water)

¼ cup coconut butter

½ teaspoon vanilla extra, vanilla powder, or vanilla bean

¼ teaspoon sea salt

1 cup goji berries or any dried berry or raisin

Add the Brazil nuts to a food processor using an "S" blade. Continue grinding, and add the cacao powder, Maca Extreme Powder, and Simplexity®. Continue grinding, and add the sweetener, coconut butter, vanilla, and sea salt. Batter will become a wet ball in the food processor. Continue processing and add the goji berries (the berries will soak up any excess moisture). Press batter into a 9- x 12-inch pan. Refrigerate or freeze. Brownies will keep a long time.

Katharine's Super Food Fudge

Katherine Clark (Healthworkshi@gmail.com, www.kclark.biz)

Prep: 25 minutes

⅓ cup coconut oil
⅓ cup agave nectar, honey, or yacon syrup
⅓ cup cocoa butter
1 heaping teaspoon each Amazing Grass® SuperFood Green
        Powder and Simply SBGA Powder by Simplexity®
1 cup cacao powder (or ⅓ cup carob and ⅔ cup cacao)
Dash sea salt
Dash vanilla bean powder or scraped vanilla bean

Combine all dry ingredients, then adding the liquids and mixing thoroughly. Pour mixture into brownie pan and chill. Cut brownies in advance.

Chocolate Brownies

Potlucker Dawn Light, author of Dawn of a New Day Raw
Desserts, *Phoenixville, PA. Dawn also reviews books and products
that support Lifestyles of Health and Sustainability (LOHAS) at
www.dawnofanewday.com*

Prep: 25 minutes
Soak: all ingredients, overnight or 12 hours
**Dehydrate: approximately 1–2 days at 85°F or until mixture
becomes brownie/cake-like consistency (see note)**

40 raw dates, pitted and soaked
2 cups raw cacao nibs, soaked
2 cups nuts (or sesame seeds or sesame pulp: pulp is what is
        leftover after making milk), soaked
Water

Before combining the ingredients, all ingredients must be soaked
overnight.

Drain off all soaked ingredients, saving date soaking water.
Place the dates in a food processor and blend thoroughly. Add
date soak water if necessary so you can blend dates thoroughly.
Set aside in a mixing bowl. Place the cacao in a food processor and
blend thoroughly (again, add date soaking water if needed to allow the cacao to blend thoroughly). Add to the dates in the bowl.
Place the nuts or seeds in a food processor, blending thoroughly
(use date soaking water if necessary). Mix all ingredients together
in mixing bowl and combine thoroughly.

On a solid dehydrator sheet, form the batter into your preferred brownie size (1–1½ inches high). The larger the brownies,

the longer they will take to dehydrate. Dehydrate until moist on the inside and mostly dry on the outside.

The dehydrating time will vary, but should be approximately 1–2 days, depending on the climate in which you live (how hot, how cold, how humid, etc.), because the temperature will have an effect on how long it will take for your brownie to become the desired consistency.

Try varying the size of the brownies the first time that you make them and see what size that you prefer. I suggest 3-inch squares or brownie bites at 1-inch cubes.

Key Lime Pie

Katherine Clark (Healthworkshi@gmail.com, www.kclark.biz)

Prep: 35 minutes
Soak: dates, 1 hour

Filling for 8-inch Pie Shell
1 cup cashew or macadamia cream cheese, strained in sprout
        bag to firm
4–6 limes, juiced (½ cup, or to taste)
Sweetener (stevia, yacon, agave, or soaked and pitted dates),
        to taste
1 tablespoon Simply SBGA (from Simplexity®), to color
Dash salt

Combine ingredients well by hand or in food processor. Place into pie crust (see page 130) and chill until firm. Garnish as desired (I use rose petals and lime slices).

Cashew or Macadamia Cream Cheese

Katherine Clark (Healthworkshi@gmail.com, www.kclark.biz)

Soak: cashews or macadamia nuts, 1 hour

1½ cups cashews or macadamia nuts, soaked

Cover the nuts with 3 cups of water. Drain and rinse nuts in clean water. Drain well. Place soaked nuts in Vitamix®. Turn blender on and start grinding on a low-medium speed until blade does not engage nuts. Then start adding water slowly.

Add up to 2 cups water slowly with blender running on medium-high speed until the nuts are creamed.

Blend in another ½ cup of water.

Place nut crème into a clean glass container, and cover with a cloth or loose-fitting lid. Leave empty space at the top. Do not fill your container to the top. The cheese will expand as it cultures. Place out of direct sun. Let it culture until you can see small round bubbles. The cheese will swell. When the bubbles are uniform throughout the mix, the cheese is done. The culturing takes longer if it is cool, and happens faster if it is warmer (typically within 10 hours in warm weather and up to 3 days in cooler weather). You can also place in an open dehydrator to speed the process. Set dehydrator to low and leave the door open. If whey has formed on the bottom, discard. If your cheese is still very soft and moist, you can place the cheese into a mesh bag, and hang for an hour until the water drains off and you have firmer cheese. The cheese should be white and fluffy, and will smell good. Now, it is ready to use.

Pie Crust

Katherine Clark (Healthworkshi@gmail.com, www.kclark.biz)

This crust is perfect for an 8-inch pie dish.

Prep: 15 minutes
Soak: hazelnuts or cashew, 4 hours

1 cup hazelnuts or cashews, soaked and dried
1 cup flax seeds, ground
Dash sea salt
6–10 dates, pitted

Combine nuts, seeds, salt, and dates in a food processor until it forms into a ball. Press dough into pie shell and chill.

MY OWN RECIPES

_____
_____
_____
_____
_____
_____
_____
_____
_____
_____
_____
_____
_____
_____
_____
_____
_____
_____
_____
_____
_____

MY OWN RECIPES

_____

_____

_____

_____

_____

_____

_____

_____

_____

_____

_____

_____

_____

_____

_____

_____

_____

_____

_____

_____

_____

MY OWN RECIPES

MY OWN RECIPES

MY OWN RECIPES

_____

_____

_____

_____

_____

_____

_____

_____

_____

_____

_____

_____

_____

_____

_____

_____

_____

_____

_____

_____

_____

MY OWN RECIPES